Death Embraced:
Tombs and Burial Customs of New Orleans

Behind the Scenes Accounts of Decay, Love and Tradition

*To Joe and Rebekka
they took my tour
1/28/19*

MARY LaCOSTE

Mary LaCoste

Dedicated to my ever patient husband Al, my literary sister Liz and the talented experts I consulted, particularly Pat Dupuy, Billy Henry and Mary Gehman.

Artwork by Brad Dupuy, photographs by Joyce Cole, Pat Dupuy and the author.

CONTENTS

Appendices:

PREFACE

It was the old deArmas-Villarrubia family tomb which first ignited my passion for learning all there was to know about New Orleans' burial customs. The tomb is a modest but imposing edifice in St. Louis Cemetery No. 3 and bears inscriptions in French, Spanish and English. My husband, Alvin LaCoste, holds title to this, the place where his parents and scores of relatives have been interred over the past one hundred and thirty-eight years. He remembers, as a boy, cleaning and whitewashing the grave in preparation for November first - it was considered a disgrace to have signs of neglect on a family tomb on that day, the Feast of All Saints.

Visiting the tomb, I wondered about the individuals whose remains were inside. The cemetery office provided me with the names and burial dates of most of the forty-three occupants. This started my genealogical and historical search. Why burials above ground? How could the remains of so many persons be housed in a typical family tomb designed to hold two coffins? Are people still being interred this way? Are the funeral customs grotesque? Is above-ground burial sanitary or even ethical? Does the occult play a role? My investigations provided a good many answers, revealed fascinating stories and raised a host of new questions.

I was born and raised in a modern section of New Orleans. My own family, with Minnesota roots, had different traditions. My parents let it be known that they wished to be buried below ground in one of the New Orleans' modern suburban cemeteries, just as their parents and grandparents had been buried in Minnesota. There, they told me, bodies could not be buried in winter but were held for the spring thaw. At least *that* is not a problem in New Orleans. Apparently, disposal of the dead is seldom convenient, no matter the location.

My retirement occupation is as a licensed tour guide. I give a variety of tours including French Quarter walks and cemetery tours. Like most professional guides, I strive to be accurate. Lectures and training by the Friends of the Cabildo and Save Our Cemeteries organizations were helpful. I give the "standard" tours of St. Louis Cemetery No. 1, St. Louis Cemetery No. 3 and the Lafayette Cemetery. Tourists are delighted with my guided tours. Over the years, I have learned that guides, including me, have contributed to myths and inaccuracies about the history, function and usefulness of the tombs. We have relied on "hand-me-down" stories that have not been properly checked or researched. Worse, the richest and most intriguing information is often overlooked or ignored.

I was determined to learn the actual facts. It was important to find out what really went on inside the whitewashed sepulchers and more about the families and professionals involved. The plan for this book was to interview cemetery workers, embalmers, funeral directors, forensic anthropologists, religious leaders and the owners of family gravesites as well as the people who build and restore the above-ground graves. Early on, I decided not to report on the architectural styles in the historic cemeteries as there are already many scholarly books and articles on the subject. Instead, I chose to focus on customs and on practical matters.

It was important to determine if above-ground burial is efficient, good for the environment or merely a curiosity. I wanted to investigate the process of decomposition in the context of tomb burial and attempt to establish a timeline of "natural cremation," a process that is supposed to take place in them. It seemed appropriate to explore issues related to cremation and DNA preservation. I decided to limit my research, for the most part, to the burial grounds within the city of New Orleans with particular attention to family tombs.

As I explored the social aspects of local funeral practices, I traveled down paths of discovery from jazz funerals and dignified memorials to-over-the-top wakes and sports-themed caskets. For every fact checked, for every interview, there were new and unexpected revelations.

Of immense help was the Internet with pictures and data (always to be double checked). Personal interviews were rich sources of information. I was amazed how willing funeral professionals and families were to share stories and to call into question popular myths. All of this helped me write more accurate descriptions of the functioning of New Orleans cemeteries and to make realistic plans for my own future.

This book is designed in such a way that it does not have to be read cover to cover. The chapters are short to please folks, like me, who like to browse and then follow up on ideas found intriguing. Pictures, captions and the table of contents should please scanners. Scholars may wish to view the list of books and electronic sources.

Important features are the annotated list of cemeteries and the maps in the Appendix sections. Some readers may want to make a hobby of exploring historic burial grounds, if true, this modest volume can serve as a handbook. Opinions in the list are mine and I will welcome reader observation and photographs through e-mail at edprofno@aol.com.

The following chapters relate what I have discovered… so far.

CHAPTER 1

A "Typical" Tour of the Oldest Cemetery

The early morning sun shines brightly on the walls of the historic St. Louis Cemetery as the attendant unlocks the heavy wrought-iron gate. Members of a tour group wait impatiently, anxious to view the variety of tombs and monuments in what has been called "The City of the Dead." Curious, they enter, some expecting history; others, macabre adventure and tales of Voodoo.

Their guide, Miss Julie, lively but well past retirement age, says, "The French, who founded the city in 1718, had problems burying their dead. Because of a high water table, coffins buried underground would pop to the surface after heavy rains." Her audience reacts with the expected sounds of disgust. She continues, "The Spanish took over the colony in the 1760s, closed the old French cemetery, opened this one and moved the bones here. It was the Spanish who came up with the idea of above-ground burials, unique to New Orleans. Each family was asked to purchase a plot and build a house for their dead."

Gesturing with her closed umbrella, she leads the group to a family tomb tall enough to hold three coffins. Pausing for effect, she says it contains the remains of fifty-two people. Faces reflect disbelief and fascination. She offers an explanation: "In our climate, natural cremation takes place. Human remains become ashes in a year and a day. The ashes are placed in the basement of the tomb, joining the dust of ancestors. The vault is tidied up in time for the next funeral." She overcomes their skepticism by adding, "Dust thou art and to dust thou shall return."

They move on to the grave of Marie Laveau, Voodoo Queen. Julie suggests they make a wish but avoid adding to the X marks left by others. With a wink she says, "Touch the tomb, make a wish and turn around three times. Remember which way you turn because, if you need to take your wish back, you must return to New Orleans, touch the grave, and turn three times the opposite way!"

Cameras and cell phones click as a few members of the group add token gifts on top of the weathered offerings of food, drink, pennies and Mardi Gras beads they see heaped before Laveau's final resting place. "I heard that Voodoo is part of the Catholic religion here," opines a modestly tattooed member of the group. "They believe in vampires too."

Passing other groups, they approach a monumental tomb belonging to an Italian burial society. Julie gestures saying, "This is where scenes from Easy Rider were filmed - causing quite a scandal. The bishop said that no movie making would be allowed in this or any other Catholic cemetery in New Orleans. Double Jeopardy's scenes had to be shot in the city cemetery in the Garden District."

Bypassing the final resting place of Homer Plessy of Plessy vs. Ferguson fame, they enter an open space which their guide identifies as the Protestant Section. "In the old days, dead people were segregated by religion, not by race," she explains. "In more modern times, an entire Protestant cemetery was moved to make way for the Superdome sports stadium. Some say that brought a curse on the Saints football team."

Visitors to New Orleans can be introduced to historic cemeteries with guided tours like this one of St. Louis Cemetery No. 1. While a few are excellent, too many are based on mixtures of simplified history and hearsay, fiction and fact. Entertaining and somewhat informative, they satisfy the average tourist but can serve to perpetuate half-truths and misconceptions that trivialize local customs.

Tourists are aware of the saying, "Guides don't let truth get in the way of a good tale." Unfortunately, there is a human tendency to believe as true the first way a person hears a story and to resist changing ideas, even in the face of hard evidence. Perhaps that is why the historically incorrect practice of marking Xs on the Laveau tomb has persisted for so long... and so much else has been missed.

CHAPTER 2

Tombs and Cemeteries: Fact and Fable

Called the "Cities of the Dead," the old cemeteries of New Orleans have been viewed as mysterious, odd and somewhat macabre expressions of a decadent time. In truth, they have quite respectable roots. Above-ground burials are practiced in many parts of the world but are uncommon in English-speaking countries. These include the United States and Canada where British burial traditions of in-ground graves with headstones are followed. (Ironically, Great Britain is running out of space and is now encouraging cremation.)

At the time the St. Louis Cemetery was founded in 1789, public attention in the Western world was turning to cemetery reform. Authorities had begun to address problems involving the hygienic disposal of corpses. Officials in London and Paris, faced with rapidly growing populations, came up with plans.

In Paris, the most overcrowded burial grounds were closed. The bones were collected and placed in underground catacombs, the skulls and bones arranged in artful patterns which later became tourist attractions. By the early 1800s, the cemeteries of Père Lachaise in Paris and Kensal Green in London had been founded, both successful symbols of change.

Somehow this tomb in Lafayette No. 2 Cemetery was never
used, they say, but it gives a rare opportunity to view the inside
of a typical two vault family tomb with space below for ashes
and bones. Similar ones have accommodated a large number of
burials, only the most recent ones are in the top two vaults.

Are the oft repeated tales of coffins popping out of the ground factual? Could this have ever happened in the early days of New Orleans? When the very first settlers buried someone, they chose the levee along the Mississippi, but the practice was soon abandoned. When the river reached flood stage it became obvious that graves had created weak spots where water could rush through... perhaps carrying a coffin in the torrent!

Before long, the city fathers established a cemetery inside the town walls, just a few blocks from St. Louis Cathedral. Burials were in the ground both when the French ruled and when Spanish took over in the mid-1860s. In time, that burial ground became overcrowded and odorous. Occasionally, animals disturbed graves. Stories of coffins floating to the surface have never been authenticated.

After the great fire of 1788, the Spanish authorities redesigned the town. The very next year, they opened the St. Louis Cemetery. Above-ground burials in tombs, the kind used in Spain and many Spanish colonies, were encouraged, but shallow graves covered by low structures of brick were allowed. The choices were cultural as well as a way of dealing with the damp soil. The new burial ground was a welcome solution to the problem of respectful care of the dead.

The older, overcrowded graveyard continued to be used for a period of time. Eventually, it was deconsecrated and the land divided into needed building lots. The bones were moved to the St. Louis Cemetery, located at the town's edge. (The construction of a twentieth century hotel on the site of the old burial ground revealed forgotten remains.) The footprint of the newer cemetery, now known as St. Louis Cemetery No. 1, has changed somewhat over the years as streets were added and a turning basin was built for a canal that led to Bayou St. John which, in turn, led to Lake Pontchartrain.

St. Louis Cemetery in New Orleans was the only graveyard in New Orleans until after the Louisiana Purchase in 1803. Each family or organization was invited to purchase a plot and see to the erection of a suitable tomb and its upkeep. Typical family tombs had two or three coffin-sized vaults. Each vault was intended for multiple uses and a space was built beneath each tomb to hold dried remains that had been moved to make way for subsequent burials in the main vaults. Tradition held that a body should not be disturbed for at least a year but many years could pass before that vault would again be needed.

The custom of waiting one year has invited some grotesque interpretations. One recently heard version is that a ceremony is held a year and a day after burial, during which the corpse is removed and placed in a wall vault called an oven… where it is burned! Of course, such ceremonies are never held. Wall vaults do exist, but they are used for interments, not to incinerate corpses. They are called "ovens" because the openings, sometimes rounded at the top, resemble baking ovens. Originally wall vaults doubled as borders for burial grounds and provided spaces for a number of less expensive or temporary burial sites.

Stone was not available locally so bricks were used to build family tombs, cover shallow graves and construct large multi-vault structures for benevolent and burial societies called "society tombs." Local bricks were fragile. To prevent deterioration, structures made of them were covered with protective layers of lime-based plaster painted with whitewash, renewed as needed. Marble was expensive but could be imported for statues or inscriptions. Epitaphs were rarely used and only some of the names of the occupants were listed on the graves but the information was entered in cemetery records.

After the Louisiana Purchase of 1803, floods of immigrants arrived in the city. They were culturally different from the Creoles, the name given to the descendants of the earlier inhabitants of French, African, Spanish or German origins. The newcomers were

English-speakers and were, for the most part, Protestant. They complained that the only burial place was the Catholic cemetery of St. Louis, so the church added a space behind a rear wall to accommodate them. It is identified today by a bronze plaque stating "Protestant Section." Within a few years, Protestant, Jewish and non-denominational burial grounds were founded in many parts of the city (see Appendix I).

Protestants, recognizing the practicality of local traditions, built family tombs, wall vaults and multi-storied tombs for burial societies, just as the Creoles had done. Below-ground burials were accomplished by building a short wall, called a coping, around a grave, filling it with soil thus raising the level of the ground to a more desirable elevation. The term "coping" was used, according to most locals, because it was a way of coping with high water tables. While that is a nice explanation, the fact is that cemeteries in other parts of the United States use the term for short walls constructed around family plots.

Lafayette, a non-denominational cemetery, was opened in 1832 in what is now called the Garden District, upriver from the old city. It soon became the cemetery of choice in the upriver part of the city. It was noted for fashionable tombs, some modeled after monuments in the Père Lachaise Cemetery in Paris.

Today, the New Orleans area has about thirty-five cemeteries within the boundaries of the city. The oldest and most historic cemetery is, of course, St. Louis Cemetery No. 1. The number was added when St. Louis Cemetery No. 2 was opened in 1823. By the time St. Louis Cemetery No. 3 was laid out in 1854, there were cemeteries in every neighborhood.

Tennessee Williams, in his prizewinning 1947 play, *A Streetcar Named Desire*, tells of character Blanche DuBois being told to take a "streetcar named Desire, and then transfer to one called Cemeteries."

A memorable book written in 2008 by Alan Leonhard, *New Orleans Goes to the Movies,* describes the significance of that poignant scene.

Today, the streetcar bearing the name Desire has been replaced by a less glamorous motor bus. There still exists a streetcar called Cemeteries (technically the Canal/Cemeteries line). It leads to a cluster of over a dozen cemeteries where Canal Street meets City Park Avenue. This part of the city is called - what else - the Cemeteries." The area is on a natural ridge and was once part of a sparsely populated neighborhood. The water table was not a problem in this area but above-ground burial practices were followed as the tradition had become well established.

Exceptions are the Jewish cemeteries. As the Hebrew tradition calls for in-ground burial, most of the graves are of the coping style. The oldest existing Jewish cemetery, Gates of Prayer Cemetery No. 1, is among three located in the cemeteries area. Most of the other Jewish cemeteries in New Orleans are situated on relatively high ground in an area known as the Gentilly Ridge.

Today, the city and its suburbs have a variety of burial facilities including mausoleums, special gardens for cremated remains as well as lawn-style final resting places with below-ground burial sites and markers flush with the ground, handy for efficient lawn care.

The dead in New Orleans have many options.

CHAPTER 3

Decomposition, Forensic Anthropology and DNA

Above-ground burial practices were a good solution for eighteenth and nineteenth-century New Orleanians. They took less space, important in a city fast running out of dry land, as vaults could be used again and again. Tombs were sanitary, avoided the problem of soggy soil and were esthetically pleasing. Is the popular assertion true—that bodies become dust in one year when placed in tombs? Forensic anthropologists and cemetery workers agree that this is highly improbable, even impossible.

Climate, environment, time and temperature affect rates of decay of the human body. So do the condition of the remains, post-death treatment (for example, embalming, which slows down the process only a little), the container in which the body is placed and the final resting place. Left to nature, human bodies undergo changes and are reduced, ultimately, to their organic and mineral elements. You might say that human bodies are biodegradable.

The emerging field of forensic anthropology has made a science of noting rates of decay of human corpses as a tool in solving crimes.

It is no longer true that "dead men tell no tales." Murders and missing persons cases have been solved by combining the careful examination of remains, even in advanced stages of decay, with careful police work and electronic information sharing.

Public interest in this area has given rise to a new genre of crime novels and popular television programs such as *Bones* and *Crime Scene Investigation or (CSI)*. A spin-off of *NCIS* set in New Orleans recently featured a night-time scene in which people strolled through the Garden District Cemetery. Graves were bedecked with flickering candles. Of course this led to the wonderfully dramatic finding of a body. In real life, this cemetery is locked at 3pm, as is the custom in most of the city, and candles are not put on graves. That practice, however, can be found along the bayous and in rural parts of South Louisiana.

Mary Manhein, of Louisiana State University, is one of the nation's leading forensic anthropologists. Among her resources are data from four universities which maintain "body farms:" private sites in which donated corpses undergo decay outside in the open air or in planned environments. The largest of these is the Forensic Anthropology Center of Texas State University (FACTS). From time to time, information is collected by medical students, criminal justice majors and their professors. Timelines of decay are produced and the roles of trauma, insects, bacteria and weather are recorded, data which is helpful in determining time of death in police investigation of murders.

Known affectionately as "The Bone Lady," Manhein and her staff work tirelessly to solve crimes and identify corpses. She has written authoritative books on the subject as well as a mystery novel, *Floating Souls: the Canal Murders,* in which forensic anthropology plays an important role. In a telephone interview in 2013, she stated that, to her knowledge, a New Orleans tomb has never been the scene of a crime. The 1999 movie, *Double Jeopardy,* which features a fictional murder attempt involving a tomb, is not true to life... yet.

A corpse will undergo predictable changes after death. Unless there are unusual circumstances, it will progress through various stages of rigor mortis, putrefaction and drying until there is little left but bones or bone fragments. There are systems of classification of these stages. A brief Internet search can produce pictures of each stage, if one can stand to look at them.

Another look at the changes that can take place after death is in a book called *Stiff: the Curious Lives of Human Cadavers*, by Mary Roach. Strangely enough, it made bestseller lists in 2003. It is not to be read by the faint-hearted. Despite my interest in tombs, I could not finish it, but it did convince me that I did not wish to witness an embalming session. Otherwise, I tried to do fact-checking through interviews, viewing an embalming room and observing a cremation and its aftermath.

Every society has methods for the disposal of the dead. The health of the public is well served by the fact that people instinctively avoid contact with human bodies once decomposition has begun. The changes that take place in corpses are far from pretty and the odors produced are strong and revolting. Bacteria from the internal organs help break down a body. Insects speed up the process. Flies lay eggs that hatch into the body destroyers we call maggots. There is truth in a childhood ditty that goes, "the worms crawl in, the worms crawl out..."

The Egyptians slowed down the decay of their dead by removing internal organs and treating the rest of the body with various substances. In the past, some American Indian tribes put remains on high platforms and let carrion birds do their job. Cremation using funeral pyres is still practiced in India. Much of the world now chooses entombment, deep burial in the earth or cremation. Whatever the method employed, the natural process of decay remains hidden from view. Survivors are spared direct contact with the sights and smells of decomposition and bacterial contamination of the living is prevented.

New Orleans' historic cemeteries have below ground burials as well as above ground tombs. St. Patrick's, for example, has about half of each. All of the graves in the Jewish cemeteries are below ground like this one in Gates of Prayer.

The kinds of tales that the dead can tell are increasing as the technology of forensic anthropology takes leaps forward. Biologists have examined Egyptian mummies and determined cause of death and their health problems when alive. Thomas Jefferson has been named as the possible father of a slave's child. This was done by the examination of the DNA of descendants. Recently, the skeletons and intact bodies of Italian Renaissance notables have been studied to learn of their diseases and dietary habits - all reported in detail by Tom Mueller in the July 2013 issue of *Smithsonian Magazine*.

Information stored in the remains of people passing away today may be of importance to the health of future generations. Scientists can now determine predispositions to certain kinds of cancers and illnesses through DNA samples. More is certain to be discovered in the future. In-ground as well as tomb burial can possibly reveal some information many years after death. Not so with cremation. At the present time, experts agree that cremation by today's methods will destroy any usable DNA. Families contemplating cremation may want to consider saving a lock of hair of the newly deceased… for practical as well as sentimental reasons.

CHAPTER 4

Within the Sepulchers:
Remains, Cremains and... Surprises?

When it is time for an above-ground burial, the cemetery sexton is informed to prepare the appropriate vault in a tomb. He or his workers remove the outer tablet and break open the brick wall behind it. They dispose of what is left of the casket of the last "occupant" and bag the human remains. These are placed in a basement-like space under the tomb called the "caveau" or "receiving vault." Direct access to the caveau is from the bottom vault. Remains in upper vaults can be simply stacked in the rear or put in the caveau via the lower vault. I have not been able to verify reports that some upper vaults have special slots in the back that can act as a sort of laundry chute for bones.

After cleaning the prepared vault, the workers hang a curtain over the opening. When the funeral party arrives, they wait at a respectful distance. After the words of religion or hope are said, the coffin is lifted and slid into the tomb. The curtain is dropped and the casket can no longer be seen. Within an hour of the departure of the last mourners, the opening will be re-bricked, sealing it. Later, the enclosure tablet, frequently of marble or granite, will be put into place. It is the custom to leave the grave undisturbed until it is needed again.

Things can go wrong. Once in a while the funeral procession arrives and finds the casket too wide for the opening. A flurry of activity ensues as handles are unscrewed. If that fails, grave-side services will be postponed. It is the job of the funeral director to measure the opening and order a coffin of appropriate size. It is said among funeral directors that they will make this mortifying mistake only once in their careers.

Wood is the material of choice for tomb burial. Human bodies are over 60 percent water. As they decompose and dry, they produce water vapor that must go somewhere. If the casket is airtight, condensed water vapor can collect under the top of the coffin and rain down on the dead. Wood allows for evaporation and natural decomposition can take place.

After a year, the smelly part of decomposition should have been accomplished. There is a tradition—never a law—of waiting at least "a year and a day" before a vault space is reused. From the cemetery worker's point of view, a longer period of time is better.

Traditional tombs built the old-fashioned way have adequate natural ventilation. Until recent decades, above-ground tombs were made of bricks coated with a lime-based plaster that bonded well with the brick. The walls were protected by coats of lime whitewash, renewed as needed. Tombs made this way would keep out rain but let the bricks breathe. More modern tombs made of granite or concrete have, or should have, metal vents placed on a side near the top.

The very nature of the building materials used for older tombs may be the reason they worked so well. The alkaline properties of the plaster coating on the old bricks had a sanitizing effect. The ventilation through the walls prevented moisture buildup from the ground and from decomposing bodies. The walls may even have filtered out offending odors. Experts in restoration say that attempts to beautify old tombs with modern paints can lead to long-term damage as the tombs can no longer breathe adequately and the moisture inevitably moves toward the surface, disturbing the paint and plaster coatings.

Mummified bodies? This couldn't happen inside the traditional New Orleans above-ground tomb, or so say experts. There are a host of reasons. The climate is too humid. Despite sweltering summers, it does not get hot enough inside tombs to sterilize corpses to the extent that it could stop the relentless onslaught of bacteria from internal organs. (However, no one has successfully determined the hottest temperature reached inside a tomb in August.) Even if heat sterilization were possible, hungry insects or larger varmints would aid decomposition.

But it happens… or so it is said. Cemetery workers tell firsthand accounts of bodies that mummified. In one case, when workers opened a vault to prepare it for a scheduled funeral, they found the stiffened corpse of a man which was quite intact. Time was short so they hid it behind neighboring graves. After the service, they put the body on top of the new casket before the bricking up was done. They hoped the vault would not be needed for many years.

Is there any documentation of mummies? Not really, perhaps because sextons do not want scenarios like the one mentioned to be advertised. "Deal with the problem, don't cause a stir," is the likely reaction.

Reported to me by a close and truthful relative was her experience when she attended her uncle's funeral in the 1930s. He was being laid to rest in a space formerly used by his father. She said she observed a body covered with green grass cloth hidden behind the tomb and could see a man's foot sticking out. I wish I had asked her, when she was still alive, if she remembered whether the foot was wearing a shoe.

Vandals are taking a toll in some of our oldest burial grounds and this has led to plans to limit access to some of them. Here, someone removed bricks from a 150 year old tomb to reveal the cast iron coffin... of a child.

Individuals who leave instructions for cremation often do so with hopes of avoiding the messy stages of decomposition and of leaving a smaller carbon footprint. Is cremation kinder to the environment? The escaping moisture at the time of cremation is not a problem, but carbon dioxide and carbon particles escaping into the atmosphere and the fuel burned could add to global warming. Realistically, cremation could add about the same amount of harmful emissions as were produced by the deceased's automobile in his last months of driving.

Tomb owners, as well as people with family plots, frequently investigate the option of cremating the deceased's remains and placing the container of ashes in the family grave. The Roman Catholic Church had long opposed cremation but, since the 1960s, has allowed it as long as the ashes are treated in a respectful manner. The Church has even given nuns the option of cremation. Some Christian denominations, other than Catholic, have begun to provide niches in their church buildings as permanent resting places for urns.

If a family grave is not available or desired, and survivors do not want to purchase a designated space in a church or mausoleum, the problem of what to do with the ashes presents itself. Many church leaders would not consider it appropriate or respectful to put grandpa on the mantelpiece or in a closet. Scattering cremains has become fashionable but seems, to many, an irreligious act. Patrons of bars have come up with exotic suggestions for where and how to do the scattering. Making use of the Algiers Ferry seems appropriate to New Orleanians. Unfortunately, not all mourners consider wind direction… to the dismay of fellow passengers.

People who have been tasked to do the scattering are surprised that they do not look like ordinary ashes but are whitish gray in color and more granular than expected. After cremation, large bone pieces remain. These are placed into a chopper at the crematorium which reduces them to smaller particles that are mixed with the ashes. The result resembles kitty litter. Some folks want the material made a part of jewelry or shot into space. Companies exist to take care of these wishes... for a price.

Ironically, whether cremation is chosen or the body is allowed to undergo the long, natural process of decomposition, the end result is the same: the earthly body, no longer needed by the person, is ultimately reduced to bone fragments and to... dust.

CHAPTER 5

Voodoo, Vandals and... Vampires?

Voodoo has cast a spell on New Orleans. There are ghost and Voodoo tours every night attended by tourists and locals alike. Several French Quarter shops sell charms and Voodoo dolls. The fast-growing Voodoo Music Festival, held every October, has little to do with Voodoo but much to do with cutting edge music. There are, however, a few local practitioners and individuals who adhere to the old beliefs - beliefs that have been greatly exaggerated by the entertainment industry and by tour guides.

Voodoo was little known in the early years of New Orleans. The Spanish were not tolerant of any religious systems other than their own. (Remember the Inquisition?) Those who practiced African-based beliefs found it best to hide it by using Catholic statues which they renamed for Voodoo spirits. This led some to believe that, in New Orleans, Voodoo is a branch of Catholicism. Visitors too often think that anything is possible in a city that allows drinking in the streets!

The newly restored tomb of Marie Laveau, called Voodoo Queen, is again attracting "X" marks by people making wishes, a practice that is illegal and not part of Voodoo ritual. Located in St. Louis No. 1, it attracts a large number of visitors, most of whom respect the grave and make wishes without defacing it.

Increased interest in Voodoo came with the waves of refugees from the revolution in Haiti that began in 1791. The revolution so soured Napoleon on the Western Hemisphere that he decided to sell Louisiana after briefly regaining it from the Spanish. That transaction is known in history books as the great Louisiana Purchase of 1803. In the space of a year, New Orleanians were Spanish subjects, became French for less than a month, and then found themselves citizens of the United States. Those were exciting but confusing times.

Perhaps wanting more control over their lives, some people turned to the rituals of Voodoo, not only the slaves, but other segments of the population as well. People of all backgrounds - black and white, rich and poor, appealed to Voodoo Queen Marie Laveau for help in matters of love, finance or power. Some say she was the most powerful woman in the city for much of the 1800s. After she died, they continued to seek her help by making wishes on her tomb... and still do it today.

The details of Laveau's life (1794-1881) remain murky despite the many books and articles written about her. It seems that she grew up Catholic under Spanish rule. As an adult, she learned the details of Voodoo from a Haitian refugee and became moderately wealthy from those seeking her aid. She did not, however, completely cut her ties with the Church and, according to popular tradition, retired, went to Mass regularly and helped the poor. She left the business to her daughter who closely resembled her and who is buried in St. Louis Cemetery No. 2. Some hold that it is the other way around and the real Marie Laveau is in the newer cemetery.

Late one night, in December of 2013, someone climbed over the wall of the locked St. Louis Cemetery and painted Marie Laveau's tomb a bright shade of pink! The pink was removed and the tomb renovated. The paint was not the first act of desecration. For many years visitors have been scribbling triple Xs on it while making wishes. Periodically, members of the Tour Guide Association attempt to erase them and apply fresh coats of whitewash - but the faux custom continues with new marks, even though there is nothing in Voodoo lore to suggest such a practice.

What we now call Voodoo was one of several sets of spiritual practices and beliefs brought to the Americas with enslaved persons from West Africa. Under different names, it can be found in many locations including Brazil, the Caribbean Islands and even in staid Philadelphia, where it has the name "Santeria." The practices are not uniform from place to place or even within a region. Experts who have made a study of it seldom agree. A few compare it to American Indian beliefs of spirits in objects governed by a single overriding power. (Monotheism?)

One aspect of Voodoo that seems not to be found in Louisiana is the Zombie, the walking dead. If they are here, no one talks about them. (Umm.) Locals have suggested that they have been vanquished by Vampires, the kind popularized by New Orleans-born author Anne Rice. People are thrilled by her novels, including *Interview with the Vampire* and the movie version with Brad Pitt. They love to seek out sites in the Lafayette Cemetery where her fictional characters are supposed to be buried.

Vandals and thieves are more of a threat to historic cemeteries than Voodoo, tourists or the passage of time. Superstition and fear deter many an act of vandalism but do not stop thieves who have found ready markets for statues and wrought-iron gates stolen from graves. In the past decade there have been arrests of the worst of the dealers in stolen artifacts and it has become less of a problem... or the best has already been taken.

Recently a man was arrested for pretending to be a licensed guide and removing loose bricks from neglected tombs in the old St. Louis Cemetery. He had hoped to be rewarded with generous tips by letting curious visitors peer inside family tombs and take photographs. In one case he made an opening that revealed the sad sight of a cast iron coffin… child sized.

Vegetation may be more of a menace than vandals. Plants, even lovely sub-tropical vines, are slow-acting, relentless destroyers of monuments. Seemingly built to last an eternity, tombs will last only as long as they are properly maintained. Ferns may look pretty but all plants force roots into mortar, creating and enlarging cracks and leading to disintegration over time. The old customs of families cleaning off vegetation and regularly applying fresh coats of whitewash are being practiced less and less as the oldest cemeteries fall into decay. Many original families have died out, moved away or have simply forgotten the graves.

There are other forces that threaten final resting places. It is hard to imagine any threats more destructive that the terrible powers of storms or of floods. Hurricane Katrina brought both to South Louisiana.

CHAPTER 6

Hurricane Katrina Devastates The Living and The Dead

Hurricane Katrina slammed into Louisiana and Mississippi at the end of August, 2005. Over sixteen hundred lives were lost, thousands of family homes were ruined and more than half of the city of New Orleans was devastated by the floodwater surge that followed the storm. The tidal surge brought sea water from the Gulf of Mexico, through Lake Borgne and into Lake Pontchartrain, the large body of water bordering the city on the north.

Contrary to popular belief, the levees at the Mississippi River and Lake Pontchartrain held fast at New Orleans. The culprits were the city's canals leading to the lake. The lake was filled almost to the top of the lake's levee and the water backed into the canals. Their weaker levees were topped by walls that gave way in several areas as the unexpectedly high water pressed against them. The most catastrophic damage occurred near the canal breaks, as happened in the Ninth Ward, Lakeview and Gentilly neighborhoods.

Homes near the breaks were swept off their foundations. It took almost two days for water from the breaks to flood the center of the saucer-shaped city. Fifty percent of buildings in New Orleans had significant flooding. Higher lands on natural ridges or near the river or lake were spared. Salt water lingered for three weeks until the drainage canals were repaired and the pumps were finally able to drain the city. Available on the Internet are vivid chronologies and maps that tell the terrible story.

Almost all of the historic New Orleans cemeteries were flooded by the intrusion of dirty water. The flood levels varied from a few inches in some sites, such as the old St. Louis Cemetery, to four and five feet in others. In time, the graves dried and the exteriors were cleaned. A lingering after-effect was rust on the iron fences surrounding grave sites. That the cemeteries were historically established on slightly higher grounds saved them from the fates suffered by the worst-hit neighborhoods—where homes were flooded to the attics.

The Beth Israel Synagogue in Lakeview had over six feet of water that severely damaged all seven of the precious Torah scrolls and three thousand prayer books. These were buried according to Jewish tradition in a Jewish cemetery in Gentilly. Historic Torah scrolls from all over the United States were donated to help replace the loss. For several years following Katrina, the Beth Israel congregation shared synagogue space with a host congregation in nearby Jefferson Parish. The members now have their own house of worship, built near the one they had been sharing. The original building was renovated and eventually sold as a medical facility.

The cemeteries within the city limits were not located near the canal breaks and so received only relentless, slow-moving water that did not break open tombs... or raise the dead. Not so fortunate were the parishes (counties) closer to the Gulf. They received the brunt of the tidal surge when it passed east of New Orleans.

St. Bernard Parish and rural areas east and south of the city had tombs that were severely damaged or toppled. In some cases, the coffins within were expelled by the force of the water. For weeks after the storm, caskets and remains were discovered far from where they had been buried. Great care was taken to identify the bodies for reburial. Volunteers and forensic anthropologists aided in the effort. Details and graphic photographs can be found on the Internet by searching "Katrina and Cemeteries."

Could this happen again the same way? The U.S. Army Corps of Engineers claims it won't... at least *inside* the city. They say New Orleans is now protected by stronger levees and by floodgates built where each canal meets Lake Pontchartrain. Offering some protection are the sixty or so miles of wetlands south of New Orleans that can continue to soften blows from direct hits - if the problem of the ongoing erosion of those wetlands can soon be solved.

Drawing little public attention among the many terrible events following Katrina were the fates of funeral homes and the people who operate them. Many of their facilities suffered severe damage at a time when mortuary services were urgently needed. Overwhelmed by the large number of Katrina-related deaths, they attempted to meet the challenges, facing exhaustion and sharing resources and buildings as best they could. Even so, the dead had to wait.

Suffering great losses from the storm, for example, was the family that owned Rhodes Funeral Homes, Inc. Of their five locations, only the ones in Baton Rouge and Gretna did not take on water. Badly flooded were the ones on Claiborne Avenue, Chef Menteur Highway and the newly redesigned flagship facility on Washington Avenue. It had eight feet of polluted salt water in the once-lovely grand pavilion, chapel, offices and behind the scenes areas.

One employee described what had happened. "As Katrina approached, we took the precaution of moving eight coffins, with bodies scheduled for burial, and placing them on top of pews in the chapel. We thought they would be safe in the unlikely event of flood.

After the storm, no one could enter that part of the city for three weeks." Photographs taken of the aftermath showed water stained coffins being carried out by three generations of the Rhodes family and their staff members, all wearing masks. Then the hard work of cleaning and rebuilding began while the Rhodes team attempted to properly provide services out of the two remaining mortuaries.

As the funeral-related businesses in New Orleans began the slow process of recovery, they realized that the catastrophic flood and the unidentified dead must be respectfully remembered. They set about the task of planning a memorial.

CHAPTER 7

Katrina Memorial?
What Katrina Memorial?

Within the old Charity Hospital Cemetery, and visible from Canal Street, is a little-known memorial dedicated to those who lost their lives in Katrina. It is also the final resting place of eighty-six bodies that remained unclaimed after the storm, almost half of them unidentified. Well-designed, inspirational and lovely, the memorial is nestled among the dozen cemeteries clustered at the end of the Canal Streetcar Line. It is a memorial that almost did not happen.

The fact that it became a reality on the third anniversary of Katrina - August 29, 2008 - was due to the perseverance of many people and an extraordinary final push to completion by the city's funeral directors and by the coroner. They deemed it inappropriate to let the bodies remain any longer in a refrigerated warehouse. They cared.

The quietly beautiful the Katrina memorial centers around the "eye" of the storm, here represented by a black granite obelisk engraved with a birds-eye view of the memorial with walkways representing the paths of hurricane winds. They are encircled by mausoleum structures holding the remains of unclaimed and unidentified storm victims.

One million dollars of FEMA money had been set aside by the city for a suitable memorial and for the burial of unclaimed bodies. Nothing happened until encouragement came in the form of donations, including one of $100,000 from the Funeral Service Foundation, an arm of the National Funeral Directors Association. The African-American funeral directors of New Orleans, impatient and unhappy with the delays, took the lead in soliciting funds and demanding action. Matthews International Corporation was contacted to design a suitable memorial, secure local input and order materials.

Work began in earnest in May 2008, less than three months before the target date of August 29. Much had to be done. The land in the front portions of the old Charity Hospital Cemetery, which has long served as a potter's field, was carefully cleared. Permits were sought and granted. Moneys had to be set aside to provide for future upkeep by Louisiana State University, the title holder of the land.

Six mausoleum-like structures were completed and landscaping begun. A monument symbolizing the eye of the storm was the centerpiece of the design with walks curving out from it like the paths of encircling hurricane winds. Despite all obstacles, it looked as if it would be completed and the dedication would be held on time. As the date neared, Scott Anthony of the Funeral Service Foundation flew in from New York to take part in the ceremonies. He was proud of the role funeral directors from across the United States had played through their support.

Hearses to carry each of the bodies were loaned by funeral homes in and near New Orleans, free of cost. Men and women from the funeral industry volunteered to drive the vehicles and act as pallbearers to carry the sealed metal coffins into the memorial cemetery. Arrangements were made for speakers, a jazz funeral procession and the ringing of bells at the exact time of the first canal break at 9:28 am. Reporters from the national and local press were alerted.

Disaster! By August 28th Hurricane Gustav was in the Gulf of Mexico and New Orleans was in the projected path! Evacuations had begun. Citizens, their emotions still raw from the terrors of Katrina, were leaving in droves. Would the August 29th dedication have to be cancelled? The planners would not let that happen. Led by the dedicated ladies of the funeral industry, such as Sandra Rhodes Duncan and C.C. Johnson, they pulled it together with some minor changes and an abbreviated jazz procession.

At the memorial site on August 29th, the bells did ring at 9:28, echoing faint sounds of ringing across the city. Mayor Nagin led the gathering in prayer as the last bodies were put into place to the sound of Ken Ferdinand's trumpet playing "Amazing Grace." There was a soul-stirring hymn sung by Jonte Short and an impromptu trumpet performance by Coroner Frank Minyard as those gathered dried tears from their eyes.

Retired Lt. Gen. Russell L. Honoré, a Katrina recovery hero, was there to address the gathering, which included a few members of the general public, religious and political figures as well as the funeral professionals, relieved that their job was now done. An officer of a national funeral directors association was there. One major donor was barely able to catch a plane to his home state before the airport closed in advance of the hurricane.

Louis Charbonnet remembers the long, solemn line of hearses that transported the bodies from the storage warehouse to the memorial, the last one in a glass-sided hearse of the kind used in jazz funerals. A rose was placed on each casket as it was interred. The once-neglected remains were, at last, treated with dignity.

It was expected that the dedication would have full national as well as local coverage, but there was almost none. Reporters had bigger stories to follow. For several days, all focus would be on the new hurricane threat. The memorial dedication that should have been front page news was overlooked, then forgotten—even when Gustav went elsewhere. That is why, today, so few New Orleanians know of the existence of the graves or of the beautiful memorial.

The Katrina National Memorial Park is indeed impressive. Weeks after the dedication, the planned walkway and landscaping were completed. The walkway design reminds visitors of a labyrinth inviting them to stroll and to meditate. The six rectangular structures containing the crypts are faced with black granite that reflects the occasional visitor following the pathways. The large granite stone rising from the "eye" of the hurricane is inscribed with words of inspiration and explanation. Other markers identify the funeral directors and others who played parts in planning the memorial and seeing that it became a reality.

The Katrina Memorial is a suitable place to meditate and remember the terrible losses of the storm. It remains open each day to anyone who cares to reach in and unlatch the iron gates to the Charity Hospital Cemetery on Canal Street and walk a few feet into the recent past.

CHAPTER 8

Galloping Remains and Vanished Cemeteries

The first African-American Mayor of New Orleans, Ernest "Dutch" Morial, died suddenly at age sixty. That was twenty-five years ago. He was buried in his family's tomb in St. Louis Cemetery No. 1, the highlights of his remarkable career recorded on the grave. The tomb happened to be located right next to the much-visited and frequently abused tomb of Marie Laveau. It was not an ideal place to remember Morial, one of the city's most prominent leaders.

The family, including his wife and a son who had also served as Mayor, had a new, more elaborate family tomb built in St. Louis Cemetery No. 3 in 2014. The new tomb was of fine granite, not plastered-over brick like the old one, and was much larger. His remains were moved and, on the anniversary of his burial, it was blessed by leaders of several religious congregations.

History is replete with accounts of the relocation of bodies or body parts. Louis IX, the sainted thirteenth-century king of France (for whom the St. Louis Cathedral is named) died while on the Eighth Crusade. In those days, as in earlier times, it was important to bring the bodies of fallen leaders home. To make the task easier, the flesh was removed from his skeleton by boiling. His brother sent the heart to the Basilica of Monreale in Palermo, Sicily, where it remains today. His bones were brought to France and eventually placed in the Church of Saint-Denis, the final resting place of other kings of France. These remains, except for one finger bone, disappeared at the time of the French Revolution.

British General Pakenham died at the battle of New Orleans in January of 1815. His internal organs were removed to slow down decomposition (buried, legend says, under a giant pecan tree that never again produced) and the rest of him was sent to his family estate in Ireland for burial. As this was before the invention of embalming or refrigeration, his body was sent across the ocean in a barrel of rum. Arsenic was added to the rum, goes a popular story, so sailors on the ship would not drink it. More likely, it was to act as a preservative.

Louis William Valentine DuBourg was the Apostolic Administrator of the Catholic Church in New Orleans at the time of the Battle of New Orleans. He presented the laurels of victory to General Andrew Jackson on the threshold of the St. Louis Cathedral on January 28, 1815. Later that year he was appointed Bishop of Louisiana, which at that time included Missouri. Uncomfortable with local church politics and the St. Louis Cathedral rector, Pere Antoine, he took up residence in St. Louis. On his rare visits south, he would stay in quarters provided for him at the convent of the Ursuline Sisters. He died in France where he is buried... but, presumably at his request, his heart was sent in a silver box to be interred with the Ursulines in New Orleans.

The remains of the early Ursuline Sisters have also logged travel time. They accompanied the nuns in their moves from the French Quarter to the Ninth Ward in the 1820s and then, a century later, to their present location, the Ursuline Academy on State Street. Bishop DuBourg's heart went too. It is in the sisters' mortuary chapel, a brick building in a quiet inner courtyard of their grounds. Among the names on the walls is that of Bishop DuBourg along with the names and dates of the nuns who have died over the years since 1727, the year the sisters first came to Louisiana and opened the oldest continually operating school for girls in the United States.

The Ursuline Academy campus has a larger chapel open to the public with a private wing for the use of the nuns and the students. On the wall near the altar is a carved wooden container with doors that, when open, display a collection of bones that were once parts of sainted persons, some of whom lived hundreds of years ago. Many Roman Catholic churches have collections of bone fragments and items that once belonged to saints. Called "relics," they are to remind the faithful of heroic and holy lives.

Church officials admit that authentication of any relic is difficult and are anxious to avoid past scandals involving the sale of relics, scandals that may have contributed to the success of the Protestant Revolution. Perhaps this may be why the remains of Blessed Francis Seelos, a New Orleans candidate for sainthood who died caring for yellow fever victims in 1876, were taken to Rome in 1999 for examination by experts before they were returned to his local shrine with pomp, ceremony and - of course - New Orleans-style jazz funeral music.

St. Louis IX, the King of France mentioned above, acquired a relic in 1238 of such importance that he had the famed Sainte-Chapelle in Paris built to house it. The relic was a crown of thorns that was thought to be the one that Jesus wore. Unfortunately, in those days, there were no certificates of authenticity. The crown of thorns was considered second in importance only to the lost but never found Holy Grail, the one used in the Last Supper and the theme of a host of literary works and dramas such as the 2003 mystery novel, *The Da Vinci Code.*

Echoes of the desire for relics may be similar to the passion many people have today for collectables and souvenirs. They pay high prices for items that once belonged to celebrities or are connected to important events. Interesting examples are shown on television shows like *Antiques Road Show* and *Pawn Stars*. Perhaps more like the religious relics of old are products available today like wearable jewelry made from cremated remains. Thus the bereaved can take a piece of a loved one wherever they go!

In New Orleans, corpses of ordinary citizens, not just celebrities, have been moved around. Of course, it was necessary for bodies interred in New Orleans-style above-ground tombs to make one final trip from their vault to the caveau (basement) below, but the traveling went further than that. An example is the DeArmas-Villarrubia tomb in St. Louis Cemetery No. 3, where there have been several relocations. My husband is the current title holder and has a list of the names and dates of persons who have been buried there. (A fictionalized history of that tomb can be found in a later chapter.)

Between 1941 and 1954, four Villarrubias, all male, were moved at different times to other parts of the cemetery, and none to the same new "address." In each case, more than a year elapsed between death and disinterment. Why were they moved? Family feuds? A need to upgrade accommodations? As all the family members from that era have passed away, it remains a mystery.

In the years between 1955 and 1992, six more family members were buried but stayed put... well, almost stayed put. A great aunt was interred in a metal coffin, which is against cemetery regulations. Later it was removed. Her remains should still be the tomb or, more precisely, in the space below the tomb, where they would have joined the ashes and bones of former occupants. Among the last six burials were my husband's beloved parents and aunts. No one has been placed there since 1992 and future interments will likely be of cremated remains of family members. The old family tomb may be my future address.

Lost to history are the Bayou St. John Cemetery burials recorded from 1835 until 1844. Since 1880, no trace of this record has been found. Was it swallowed up by a swamp? Does it lie beneath a roadway or under Cabrini High School? Future archaeologists may one day solve that mystery. If they do, there may be some remarkable discoveries because the suspected locations have "gumbo mud" which has remarkable preservative qualities.

Entire cemeteries can be bought and sold. This has happened several times in recent years in New Orleans but was not unknown in the distant past. The Louisa Street Cemetery was purchased in the 1840s by Don Jose "Pepe" Llulla, a fencing master known for his success in affairs of honor - duels. A popular tour guide tale says that he needed a burial ground for his numerous victims. The less exciting fact is that he invested in real estate and this was one of his more successful ventures.

At some point in time, the graveyard acquired the name "St. Vincent de Paul Cemetery" even though it never belonged to a church. (A cemetery with a similar name is owned by the Catholic Church and is in another part of the city.) In recent years, it was purchased by Service Corporation International, the largest holder of cemetery property in the U.S. It is in active use today. As with all cemeteries, the graves within them remain the property, with some limitations, of the individuals who own the titles to each of them.

Not only have individuals been relocated, but whole New Orleans graveyards removed! The first was the closing of the old French graveyard and the transfer of bones to St. Louis Cemetery No. 1. Gates of Mercy, founded in 1828, was the first Jewish cemetery in what is now New Orleans. It was in active use for only a few years and was demolished in 1957, the remains reinterred in Hebrew Rest No. 1 Cemetery. The space is now a playground.

On the twentieth anniversary of his death, the remains of former New Orleans mayor were moved to a new tomb in St. Louis No. 3. His remains had been in St. Louis No. 1 in a less appropriate grave located next to that of Marie Laveau.

Gates of Mercy was not the only cemetery to become a playground. The other was the Duverje private cemetery in Algiers, from which remains and a tomb were moved to Metairie Cemetery in 1917. As the tomb was thought to be built before the founding of Metairie Cemetery, it is has been regarded as Metairie's oldest tomb. There has been disagreement about that point.

The most dramatic cemetery move occurred in the 1950s. It was the closing of the Girod Street Cemetery, the city's first Protestant cemetery. Founded in 1822, it was located on Girod Street in what had become a business area. Progress and worsening deterioration led civic leaders to demand that it be torn down and legal proceedings were taken to accomplish the destruction.

Families were asked to reclaim remains. Many of those left were interred in the Protestant section of St. Louis Cemetery No. 1 or Hope Mausoleum. The Girod Street Cemetery was never segregated, but when it was closed, the remains of all African-Americans were sent, for reasons unknown, to the suburban Providence Park Cemetery which serves mostly African-American families.

Room was needed for the fast-developing downtown area and the Girod Street Cemetery was on valuable land. A good way to understand the conditions leading to the closing of the old graveyard is to read the first-person account of Louis Lavedan, age 81, in the following chapter.

CHAPTER 9

The Boys in the Girod Cemetery...

A True Account by Louis Lavedan

WWII had recently ended, the troops were coming home, shortages were becoming a thing of the past and there was a "We can do anything" attitude in America, especially among the returning forces entering the workforce. This new wave was bound to clash with the culture of New Orleans at the time. Chep Morrison was the new Mayor; the Old Regular Democrats had just been ousted. This was the period of change: New Main Library; New Supreme Court Building; New City Hall; the word was "out with the old—in with the new and latest."

The Girod Street Cemetery, in its greatest days, was the place for the Protestants of New Orleans to be buried. It followed the New Orleans above-ground tradition of walled cemeteries including vaults in the walls, large tombs of the societies, monuments to the dead, iron fences around some of the wealthier tombs, and statues. But the Girod Street Cemetery had long passed its greatness and it had deteriorated into almost ruin. The church that was owner and caretaker could do little to improve its blight. To get there you had to walk through some rundown neighborhoods. The city had passed it by.

Now my friend Joe and I (about 13 or 14 years old) were into history—he was a descendant of the pre-Civil War aristocracy. We, even as teenagers, could visit all sorts of cultural places in the French Quarter by his name alone. We were allowed into the main library stacks without supervision on his name. And we found out about the Girod Street Cemetery.

The whole area around Girod Street, South Rampart, Tulane and Poydras Streets, was just right for renewal—a new CIVIC CENTER. The latest in modern buildings. A concentration for government, culture, and, what was just starting, interest in large scale sports. Everything in the area had to go—leveled to the ground—for the glorious new! And that included the Girod Street Cemetery.

So my friend and I took a streetcar to Lee Circle and walked through some real rundown areas—yes, we were nervous—and arrived at the cemetery. On the side of was what was once the gate was the sexton's house with no sexton. So we entered the cemetery—two teenagers just walking into the Girod Street Cemetery just to look around. No one stopped us.

The place was a mess. Many of the tombs and vaults had been opened. The remains in them were as they were when buried. The bricks closing the vaults had been removed, probably by thieves trying to find jewelry or valuables. The bones remained. There were large mausoleum structures that were built by burial societies (remember there were no insurance companies then). They cared for the dead and, in many cases, the living survivors. These were great even in their decay— what they must have been in their glory! We could see this even as wandering teenagers.

We found an iron coffin that had been violated. The lid was not on. We found it in one of the open vaults, filled with water up to the edge. At first it looked almost like a glass liner but it was just water. Were there still the remains of someone under the water? We decided to pass on this—but the thought remains even to this day. Who was this person? Did the family think that they were secure with their iron coffin? Was the family also buried in Girod Street Cemetery?

We went home, but the cemetery remained in our memories. All those bones. All that destruction. Now, my friend lived in an area with woods behind his house and he had found the complete bones of a cat. With the help of medical texts, he had reconstructed the cat's skeleton. We talked about what we had seen—and slowly an idea developed! We would create a complete skeleton from the remains in one of the open vaults in Girod Street Cemetery. We wouldn't be opening any sealed place. How to do it?

Our big plan: Get a shopping bag, the kind you could buy in many stores on Canal Street for 5-10 cents, the ones that were about 2 ½ feet deep and 1 ½ feet wide, that had the twisted paper handles. Go into the cemetery and find some good bones and fill up the bag. Cover the top of the bag with newspaper. Go home in the streetcar.

We were interested. We didn't just read about it on our iPods—we did it. Well, we carried through with our adventure. We went back to the cemetery, past the sexton's house, found a "good" open vault, filled up the shopping bag, covered it with newspaper all neat, and went home in the streetcar without anyone paying us any attention.

We knew that we didn't have a complete skeleton, but the rest would come. Right now, we had to start the assembly process. First the bones required cleaning and identification. We got out my mother's large wash tub and filled it with water and bleach.

But that's when the cadaver hit the fan. My mother wanted to know why we needed the large wash tub, and one thing led to confession. She acted much like the scenes from the silent movies where heroine lies there waiting for the train, making all kinds of helpless gestures. My father was called in to do the screaming. All the bones were put in a safe place. The bleach was thrown out. The wash tub was returned to the laundry room and my parents talked about what to do with the bones.

They decided that to bury them in the back yard would not be the right thing (they were right since the property was converted into the parking lot for a Wendy's years later). A final plan was successfully executed. After 5p.m., when the stores were closed and all was quiet at Southern Train Station (at that time it was on Canal Street, not far from the old cemetery), *my parents drove along the front of St. Louis Cemetery No. 1, stopped and threw the bones up on top of the wall vaults.*

All went well. We never gathered any more bones. No one ever complained about the bones on top of the vaults. After so many years the Protestants and the Catholics are once again united. Did anyone ever find the remains on the top of the wall at St. Louis #1? No one seems to know.

This is a real story and I will verify it.
Louis Lavedan, Retired Physicist

(The above story has been shortened and edited by Mary LaCoste. The complete transcript is delightful and is available upon request.)

CHAPTER 10

The Superdome Curse, Devil Horses and Grave Tales

A few years after the adventure of Louis and his friend, a small group of Tulane freshmen went on what they called a "scholarly search." Although they were students of architecture, not medicine, they wanted a skull—a real one—perhaps for one of their projects. What better place than the Girod Street Cemetery, now in advanced stages of decay? Since it was scheduled to be torn down, they knew bones could be easily found, no need to open graves.

Entering the old graveyard, they were horrified to see large numbers of black insect-like creatures climbing over ruined monuments. One student identified them as devil's horses, called *chevals-diable* by the Cajun people who live west of New Orleans. He said they are dark relatives of grasshoppers frequently found swarming in older Louisiana cemeteries and ditches.

The further they went in to the cemetery, the more numerous the devil's horses became, until they seemed to coat the insides of an abandoned vault. They chose a suitable skull and left the old burial ground, shaken but victorious. None of them ever went near the cemetery site again… until it was covered by parts of the Superdome and they had become Saints football ticket holders.

This leads to a popular belief in the "Curse of the Dome." After the Saints left their old home in Tulane Stadium for the Superdome, they experienced many losing seasons. It was blamed on a curse acquired by building a sports arena on top of the old Girod Street Cemetery. The fact is that only part of the Super Dome and parking lot are on the old graveyard site, but the belief persisted. The Saints lost so often that, at one point, fans wore paper bags over their heads to conceal the fact that they were devotees of such a miserable franchise. Then, in 2010, the curse was broken… and the Saints won the Super Bowl!

But was that the end of the curse? Two years later, their coach, Sean Payton, was suspended for a year for questionable reasons. Then, in 2013, there was a thirty-minute interruption of the Super Bowl game (Baltimore vs. San Francisco) in the Superdome. It came just after halftime and Beyoncé had completed her lively performance. Half the lights in the stadium went out!

New Orleans cemeteries have their share of urban myths. Have you heard the one about the lady in white who hailed a taxi one evening as she stood outside the old St. Louis Cemetery? She asked to be brought to a Royal Street address. Arriving, she asked the driver to go to her husband's upstairs apartment to get the fare. The man who answered the door informed the driver that his wife had died several years before. When they went downstairs, the cab was empty except for a lingering scent the man immediately identified as his wife's perfume. Various versions of this ghost story have circulated from Maine to California.

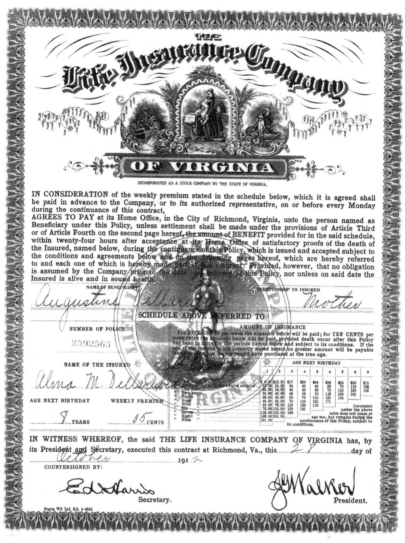

A century ago it was considered a disgrace if a family could not provide a decent funeral for a loved one. To be properly prepared, one could pay dues to a burial society or purchase burial insurance for a nickel a week. Here is page one of the 1912 policy on my husband's aunt, then a child of 8, purchased by her mother.

Fears of being buried alive peaked during Victorian times. Creative measures to prevent such calamities were invented. One plan, unverified, is said to have been used in New Orleans. It involved tying a rope to the hand of the deceased, a rope leading out of the grave to a bell. If he or she became conscious, a tug on the rope would signal a need for help… but only if someone were listening. A person had to be present, within earshot, round the clock, even late at night. Some say this late-night duty gave rise to the term "graveyard shift."

As far as it is known, such a bell never rang. However, there is a local story, unverified, of an Irish woman awaking inside her wall vault. It was in the mid-1800s. She had been buried in a shroud rather than a coffin (a cheaper alternative) and the mortar on the bricks closing her space had not yet set. She kicked and wiggled her way out, walked home and when her husband saw her at the door, he immediately died of fright.

This tale may have been the inspiration for "The Story of an Hour," written in 1894 by Kate Chopin. In that story, the roles are reversed and it is the wife who dies—not of fright but of acute disappointment that her husband has not passed away. Chopin is now considered a forerunner of feminist literature.

Embalming has become popular, some say, as a way of being sure the deceased are truly… dead.

CHAPTER 11

Caskets, Coffins, Concrete Boxes and the "Six Feet Under" Myth

Is a casket the same as a coffin? In practice, people use the terms interchangeably or, if they make a distinction, consider a casket to be a fancy type of coffin, with four sides rather than six. The word casket did not come into wide use until the twentieth century and became the term preferred by funeral directors. It was derived from the French *cassette* which means trunk or ornamented box. The word coffin, on the other hand, came from the French word *coffin*.

The newer term, casket, has given rise to a popular story that is often repeated by guides giving ghost tours when they pass the historic former Ursuline Convent in the French Quarter. They tell how, in the early years of the colony, there was a shortage of women who could become suitable wives of the settlers. Young French women were recruited to go to New Orleans by agents of the king. Each one selected was of good character but too poor to have a dowry, necessary at that time for a proper marriage. They signed contracts, were given dowries, funds and free passage to the New World. While this is not documented, they probably lived at the convent of the Ursuline Sisters until suitable marriages were arranged.

The girls' dowries, which included household items, were carried to the new world in trunks called *cassettes*. Soon the ladies were referred to as the *filles à la cassette* or "casket girls." Many locals today claim descent from them. So far, most of the story is accurate. Then, in the early 1900s, the word "casket" came to be used as a synonym, or euphemism, for coffin. (You see where this is leading!) Today, a story told on ghost tours states that the casket girls brought coffins with them, and in them were the dust of vampires... and so, goes one tale, is how vampires came to New Orleans!

Back when "coffin" was the only word used for a container for the dead, they were ordinarily simple and made of wood. Only the wealthy had elaborate ones. In Victorian times, cast-iron coffins came into use. Once in a great while, one of these is unearthed with a one-hundred-and-fifty-year-old corpse intact. The coffins, apparently airtight, sometimes preserved the bodies (not unlike canning), with preservation aided by the large amounts of arsenic used to prepare bodies at that time. Scientists are interested in examining these coffins when they are first opened so they can test the air for long-ago pollens and obtain information about the lifestyle of the deceased. Once opened, however, decomposition of the remains begins quickly.

Today, most families use the more up-to-date word "casket" and will acquire one from a funeral home as part of final arrangements. They can rent one, which is practical if there are cremation plans, or purchase one from a variety of models to suit their tastes or religious affiliations. For example, plain coffins made without nails are required by some Orthodox Jewish congregations. Lovely in their simplicity, they are made of wood without any metal whatsoever. Even the handles and hinges are wood.

The Benedictine monks at Saint Joseph Abbey in Covington, Louisiana, have been making simple pine coffins for many years for the use of their members. In 2007, they began selling them to the public until stopped by the Louisiana Board of Embalmers and Funeral Directors, who stated that the monks did not have the proper licenses. The U.S. Supreme Court ruled in favor of the monks, who are again hand-crafting and selling their product.

Inspired by the monks' legal victory, a local entrepreneur opened a shop selling caskets in 2013, in a popular suburban mall. Bearing the name *'Til We Meet Again*, it offers coffins customized to a person's hobby, lifestyle or favorite sports team. One of four operating in the United States, the shop is doing well and, said the manager, has not been plagued by crank calls but is occasionally visited by giggling teens.

A bigger problem for his business has been a legal challenge by the National Football League. The NFL voiced objection to the use of the Saints team colors and symbols on caskets, citing infringement on their intellectual property. They have not pursued that claim recently, perhaps fearing negative publicity.

Like the funeral homes, it can supply special oversized sized caskets or order extra-narrow ones for use in tombs that have unusually small openings. All sizes can be customized to suit the buyer. There are special coffins for use in cremation that are more combustible than typical coffins. All purchases can be delivered to the designated funeral parlor, payment in advance.

Urns for cremated remains are a big part of the business. Some have accessories so that cremains can be shared or put into jewelry-like novelties that can be worn. Newly popular is a biodegradable urn with a seed inside. Those with an interest in nature may like the idea of being turned into a plant or tree.

Environmentalists may approve of coffins made of wood because of their biodegradable nature. Leaving even less of a carbon footprint, they say, are containers made of bamboo, woven rattan or cardboard. Shrouds, used alone, have been suggested but have attracted very little support. As for cremation, there are mixed feelings among extreme environmentalists, many of whom who say that decomposed bodies should enrich the soil but they have not gone as far as suggesting the composting of human remains!

A wealth of information about these and other funeral customs and burial practices can be found in Houston, Texas, at the National Museum of Funeral History. According to Joyce Cole, tour guide and cemetery expert, it has among its holdings caskets that are works of art, hearses of all sorts and a model embalming room. There are special sections about celebrity burials and even one about popes. People who have visited the museum say the displays are in good taste, if a trifle unsettling.

Not featured are the coffin containers called "grave liners." Expensive, they are required for in-ground burial by some, but not all, cemeteries in Louisiana and other parts of the United States. Made of concrete or heavy plastic, they are designed to protect a casket in a grave. One might assume this is a measure to prevent contamination of ground water by a corpse but this is not the case. They are not waterproof and some have no bottom side. Cemetery owners want them as they prevent the ground from sinking over a grave when the coffin deteriorates. Grave liners simplify future lawn upkeep.

Similar to grave liners, concrete casket containers have found another use in a number of rural cemeteries in South Louisiana. Somewhat water- and airtight, they have been used as substitutes for more conventional above-ground tombs. There have been some problems in times of flood. When covered with water, these container/tombs have been known to float or rupture, expelling contents. Traditional tombs have also been violated by floods, but seem to hold up better than the grave liners used for surface burial. Severe floods have caused enough problems in coastal areas that it is now requested that identification be placed on all coffins and that bodies be tagged.

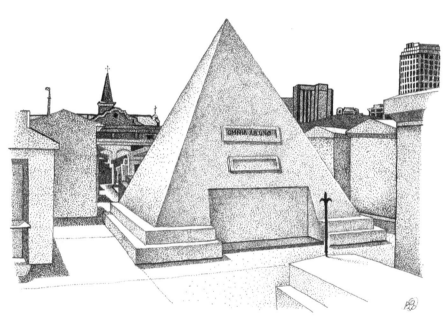

One of the newest graves in New Orleans' oldest cemetery is a pyramid owned by Nicholas Cage. Six empty crypts are inside, the outside shows evidence of kisses by fans wearing lipstick. Movie goers may wonder if there are clues to treasures hidden within.

Six feet under the ground, some would assume, is the only safe or proper way for human burial. Research, however, reveals that there is no "six feet under" rule or law. In fact, burials that deep are almost never done. Requirements for the depths of graves vary from one place to another. California requires only 19 inches of soil from the top of the grave liner. More common is a minimum of 30 to 36 inches above a coffin. Deeper burials are done if the grave is to accommodate additional burials over time. In that case, the depth for the first burial may exceed six feet so that additional coffins can be placed on top of older ones, separated by thin layers of soil.

The phrase "six feet under" stems from a pronouncement made in 1665 by the Mayor of London at the time of a plague. He hoped that deep burial would end contamination and stop the spread of the disease. It did not, since the spread was due to fleas on rodents. Eventually, the disease ran its course but the phrase remained.

Casket or coffin; in the ground or above; it doesn't matter to the dearly departed. Funeral and burial customs are not for the dead but are for the consolation of the people left behind.

CHAPTER 12

Want to be Buried in New Orleans? Possible but Complicated

So you would like to be buried in a historic New Orleans cemetery! Nicolas Cage liked the idea so much he had a tomb built for himself in the most historic cemetery of them all. As far as we know, he has no local roots, but had the good taste to want his remains to stay in "the city that care forgot." In 2009, he managed to purchase the last two adjacent plots available in St. Louis Cemetery No. 1 and had a pyramid-shaped structure built containing six crypts.

While it is yet to be verified, his grave is rumored to be the only real estate Nicolas Cage still owns since his tax problems with the Federal Government. Others say his bad luck and bankruptcy were caused by a curse acquired when he purchased a haunted house in the French Quarter. No bodies are yet in his pyramid, but does it contain, as some suspect, clues to hidden treasures?

If not a pyramid, what sort of final resting place do you have in mind? Do you want one in a historic cemetery? Is it important for you to be buried on consecrated ground? Would you be happy with a wall vault or do you prefer a two- or three-vault, family-style tomb? Among the traditional options are below-ground graves called coping tombs. They are plots that raise the surface of the ground a foot or so above grade, the extra soil held in place by a retaining wall. This avoids any concerns about the water table while providing for single or multiple burials.

The city has several mausoleums, some of which have been added to historic cemeteries, but this practice is, some say, like putting a Wal-Mart in the French Quarter. They do, however, provide affordable interments, with prices depending on location. Perhaps you would be satisfied with a niche within a historic cemetery, many of which now have special garden areas for cremated remains and permanent repositories for urns.

How about an impressive memorial? The Metairie Cemetery has elegant examples including an outstanding one built to the specification of Ruth Fertel, founder of the Ruth's Chris Steak House chain. She was so pleased with the outcome, so the story goes, that she held a cocktail party there two years before she died. Nearby tombs honor families noted for connections to the food industry. One outstanding example is that of Al Copeland, who made millions with his Popeye's Chicken chain.

You may want to select a tomb of the most traditional type. The early tombs were constructed just as the early buildings had been: both were made of fragile local bricks protected by stucco-like substances of lime plaster. The Cabildo, located in the heart of the French Quarter, is one example. The coatings were so masterfully carved that the building appears to be made of stone. Only in the mid-1800s did stronger bricks come into use.

New tombs are being made today, this one is of concrete
with a very deep caveau below. Cheaper ones are made
of cinder blocks, expensive ones of granite. The sky is the
limit if they are designed by a recognized sculptor.

The two large Pontalba buildings that flank Jackson Square were among the first made of stronger bricks. They were built in 1850 by Madame Micaela Almonester Pontalba, a native New Orleanian who had spent decades in Paris, gathering ideas. The red bricks of her structures were brought in from Baltimore and needed no protective coatings. This "naked" brick was not favored for cemetery use and whitewashed lime plaster-over-bricks remained the primary building materials used. What was copied, however, was her use of decorative cast iron. Before that, only wrought iron, beautiful in its simplicity, had been used.

Traditional materials were the choice for tomb construction until recent decades. Maintenance is demanding with the plastered brick tombs. They must be kept protected with a lime-based whitewash applied periodically. Plants can cause problems so it is recommended that growths be removed at least once a year and fresh whitewash applied (the whitewash can have color added). Flaking plaster requires timely repair, as do marble enclosure tablets. Left to nature, the old graves will ultimately crumble.

One solution is to purchase what is called "perpetual care" from the cemetery authorities. Perpetual care is not just a New Orleans custom but is available in all parts of the United States. It is a way of assuring the upkeep of gravesites. Money is deposited with the organization owning the cemetery and the interest is used for maintenance. How "perpetual" this really is will be learned in time but, for now, it works fairly well.

Older New Orleanians may remember dutifully sprucing up family tombs, applying lime whitewash and making repairs. Members of my husband's family purchased perpetual care in the 1980s for the DeArmas-Villarrubia tomb. Now, as the oldest surviving family member, my husband owns the title. He can decide who can be buried there, but has no upkeep duties. He does check on the grave and brings flowers from time to time.

Some find it odd that there are almost no epitaphs on local tombs. Family tombs generally have a last name above the enclosure tablet. The tablet itself, often of marble, may have only a few of the names and dates of the persons buried inside. There are, however, records kept by most of the cemeteries which list the names and burial dates of occupants. This information has helped many genealogists locate obituaries and information about ancestors.

Visitors have been shocked by the poor conditions of some of the city's oldest cemeteries, forgetting that over the decades, families have moved away, died off or just lost interest in their ancestors' final resting places. The older the cemetery, the more severe the problem of abandoned tombs has become. After all, a person living today may have accumulated, over the past two centuries, more than two hundred ancestors that are buried somewhere. That means a lot of graves to keep up with! (Do the math: each generation means double the number of forbearers.)

Save Our Cemeteries (SOC) is a non-profit group of preservation-minded citizens working to solve the problems of abandoned and decaying burial sites in New Orleans. To help preserve neglected tombs, SOC has had programs for "adopting" them. Interested owners can look to SOC for information about care and repair of their property. SOC, with the help of volunteers, conducts tours, sponsors lectures and has fundraisers to support their work.

SOC lists thirty-five historic cemeteries within in the city of New Orleans. Of these, seven are administered by the Catholic Archdiocese of New Orleans and six by the city. Among the others are those owned by Jewish organizations, fraternal groups and national corporations. Each cemetery must be contacted separately when searching for a space, a painstaking task. In the past, some managers of older cemeteries were reluctant to sell abandoned properties. Chief among the reasons was the difficulty of establishing the ownership of each site. (Deeds are not recorded by city or state offices but are passed down from generation to generation to show ownership.) This seems to be changing, perhaps driven by the realization that potential income sources were being overlooked.

Some plots, tombs, copings, wall vaults and mausoleum spaces are sold directly to consumers by their owners. A check of newspaper want ads under Cemetery/Funerals will reveal a few for sale. Internet sources include Craigslist and brokers who buy and sell cemetery property in all parts of the U.S. There is a market because owners of empty or used but unneeded burial places may be moving out of town or have changed plans because of divorce. As prices have gone up, some sales will realize a tidy profit, particularly with sites considered "desirable." What if the spaces have occupants? The sellers must see that they are moved elsewhere or cremated. Some buyers may allow the former occupants to stay.

If a burial plot has been selected, the design for a new structure must be submitted for approval by cemetery administrators, as each burial ground has unique rules and philosophies. Cemetery staff may recommend builders or approved craft persons to do the work. Contractors who will build traditional-looking and other types of tombs and memorials are not hard to find, but all will insist on using modern materials.

Today's builders of new tombs and monuments can use cinder blocks but prefer reinforced concrete or granite. Some families upgrade their older tombs by having them covered with granite. In the 1920s it became popular to encase graves with granite pieces mortared together to give a fashionable stone-like look for less cost, but that practice seems to have died out.

Today, enclosure tablets are made of granite as they last longer than marble. Inscriptions are done by sandblasting rather than hammer and chisel. Latex paints (harmful to old tombs) can be used with tombs made of concrete. Although the new materials make upkeep simpler, most cemeteries now require that perpetual care be purchased for all new graves, both above and below ground.

Alfortish Memorials & Mausoleums is a New Orleans company that has made cemetery structures for more than a century. Ninety-two-year-old Daniel Alfortish still goes to work part of each day and recalls working in the family business when he was a youth of seventeen. Back then, he said, plots could be bought for under $100 and the cost of building a typical family tomb was a few hundred dollars.

By 2015, a plot for a tomb in a cemetery within the city will range from $3,000 to $20,000 or more (location, location, location). The cost of building a simple two-vault tomb of cinder blocks begins at $18,000. While not cheap, a tomb can save money for a family over the decades as there is no expense for purchasing a plot after each death. There is, however a fee for opening a tomb for new occupants, the careful moving of the remains to the rear or basement of the tomb, preparing for reuse and closing of the vault after a funeral. The amount of the fee depends on the cemetery but can be above $900. If the family wants to add an inscription to the enclosure tablet, the charge could run from $6 to $15 per letter.

The cost of a below-ground plot in the New Orleans area can range from $3,000 to over $20,000. Fees for digging the grave and closing it after interment will add $1,000 or more to the total. Then there is the concrete box to contain the casket, called a grave liner, required by most cemeteries—they start at $3,000. Additionally, it is usual to purchase a headstone or marker.

Greenwood Cemetery, one of the largest in New Orleans, does still have plots available, but stipulates that buyers build a traditional or a coping tomb constructed by their builder for a package cost (lot and structure) of approximately $22,000. They suggest building a two-coffin family tomb with the vaults side-by-side instead of the more traditional up-and-down arrangement. The plot size is the same but it makes access to the caveau simpler.

Cemetery charges, of course, are in addition to the bill from the funeral home. Payment to the funeral home includes such items as picking up the body, embalming and/or cremation services, the purchase of a casket, use of a parlor for viewing and hearse service. Both the funeral home and the cemetery expect payment in advance. After all, they cannot sue the deceased and repossession is a problem. Funeral directors, with reason, hope that a family has planned ahead and has insurance to cover expenses.

Individual ownership of graves is not the custom everywhere in the Western world. In Germany, grave plots are rented for fifty years with an option to be renewed for fifty more years. Only graves of those who died in battle are considered permanent. Other countries have the problem of running out of space for burials. Authorities in England are starting to permit new burials in abandoned plots due to the shortage of churchyard space. They are also encouraging cremation.

Arranging to be buried in New Orleans is complicated and involves research, perseverance and compromises but the resulting grave may attract many admiring tourists. Out-of-town relatives and friends could find visiting your grave a useful excuse to come to the city. Future generations may want to use the economical burial spaces it can provide. Remember, however, that no grave is absolutely permanent. Descendants may want to sell your "final" resting place. Time, flood or storm can destroy any monument.

Promises for eternity are not for this world but for the next.

CHAPTER 13

The DeArmas-Villarrubia Tomb: A Fictionalized History

Two men in tall silk hats walked into the office of Florville Foy, well-known brick mason and maker of fine tombs. They were on a solemn mission. The older man's wife had just passed away and the other man had been widowed for five years. Together, they wanted to purchase a suitable tomb to be shared by their families, and they wanted it in the beautiful St. Louis Cemetery No. 3.

The year was 1877. The Civil War and the years following had left the economy of New Orleans in ruins but these two businessmen had managed to survive. Foy described to them a tomb he had built six years earlier in St. Louis Cemetery No. 3. It had already had a series of owners yet never been used. It was on a double-wide plot, simple yet dignified, fenced, with two vaults, one above the other. Made of good materials with a strong foundation and a large caveau below, it could be of use to generations to come.

What names would the gentleman want above the tomb opening? They wanted both their family names, "M. DeArmas" for the older man followed by "Villarrubia" for the second gentleman. Michael DeArmas would have use of the top vault and Joseph Villarrubia the lower one. It was arranged that the inscriptions on the marble tablet be done by Florville Foy himself, well known for his artistry in marble. As the birthplace of both wives had been Paris, they wanted that in the inscriptions as well. The two men, with Spanish roots, were accepted members of the French Creole community and proud of their wives' origins.

Not long after Martine Augustine DeArmas was laid to rest, the remains of Isabelle Coimet Villarrubia, Joseph's wife, were moved from another location and placed into to the lower vault. His parent's remains were placed there as well, their inscriptions bearing the Spanish titles of Don and Donna. They had died many years earlier. The two widowers had done their duty: their families now had a very respectable place to go to pray, bring flowers and remember.

Tragedy struck four years later when Joseph's daughter-in-law, Emilie, died a short time after giving birth to twin babies who lived less than a day. The three were buried together in the lower vault, her in-laws by now in the caveau. The young mother left behind two young sons. One was Raoul, who became my husband's great-grandfather. Florville was called to do another inscription, the one for Emilie. It was the last to be made until the twentieth century.

Michael DeArmas died in 1881 and was interred in the top vault. He was the last DeArmas to use the tomb. Joseph Villarrubia passed away four years after DeArmas. His body was placed, as expected, in the other vault. From that point on, the Villarrubia family members continued to use only the lower space, until 1913 when they began to use the entire tomb.

Below are the inscriptions on the marble enclosure tablet as they appear today. It is signed by the first name of the tomb maker at the bottom right. There are three twentieth-century additions. Note that the two men who purchased the tomb are not mentioned. They are not forgotten as their names and burial dates are in the cemetery records along with names of all but the earliest occupants. Their wives names do not appear in the records as the record-keeping did not begin until 1881. Emilie and her babies were the first to be recorded in that tomb by the Archdiocese of New Orleans.

M. DeARMAS & VILLARRUBIA

MARTINE AUGUSTINE MARCHAND
epouse de MICHEL de ARMAS
nee a Paris France. le 6 Juin 1820
decedee a la N. Orleans le 22 Juin 1877

EDGAR J. VILLARRUBIA
1916 – 1930

OCTAVE L. CHASTANT
1911 – 1932

Mle. Magne ISABELLE COIMET
epouse de Joseph Villarrubia
native de Paris. France.
decedee a la N. Orleans le 4 Fev. 1872
a l'age de 42 ans.

EMILIE d'HEMECOURT
epouse de Raoul Villarrubia
decedee le 10 Juin 1881. a l'age de 27 ans

DON JOSE LEON VILLARRUBIA
decede le 10 Nov. 1855

Son Epouse
Donna ANTONIA GAYTE
decedee le 15 Janv. 1861

EDGAR C. VILLARRUBIA
1868 - 1950

FLORVLLE

A study of the tomb and cemetery records answered many questions but raised several more. Why were there no more DeArmas family members in the tomb? Were they childless? The men who bought the tomb were very likely business partners. Were they also relatives of the family? No connection has been found. They may have been godparents to the Villarrubia children. The only hint of a relationship was a document willing DeArmas property to a Villarrubia.

Flanking the tomb and within the iron fence are two spaces, each slightly over three feet wide, that run the length of the grave. They are covered with marble chips and bordered with a curb. In the space to the right of the tomb is a marble cross, almost four feet tall. It bears the inscription:

LOUIS W. VILLARRUBIA HUSBAND
OF EMMA PETERSON

BORN JUNE 15, 1890 DIED DEC. 1, 1929

Could he have been buried next to the tomb? Cemetery records indicate he was buried in the lower vault. Were his remains later moved to the side instead of the caveau? Was the inscribed cross the idea of his grieving widow? Cemetery records indicate that she is not buried in the tomb.

Since there were at least forty-three burials spaced over the years, could the side spaces ever have been used to accommodate remains moved from the caveau? The concrete curbing around the tomb resembles the short walls that enclose below-ground burials. Could there be bones there? Experts say this is possible but highly unlikely.

We can visualize the generations visiting the tomb over the decades of its existence. In former times it was a custom for families to visit cemeteries on a regular basis. My mother-in-law recalled Sundays when she would ride her tricycle on the pathways in St. Louis Cemetery No. 3 as older family members chatted and prayed. As an adult she described the beauty of the cemeteries when decorated for the Feast of All Saints. In 1975, her earthly remains were interred in the family tomb.

It was once considered a disgrace to be unable to provide a decent "going away" for a deceased family member. In working class neighborhoods, it was customary to have a burial policy for each person in the household. It could be paid for by the week. My husband's Aunt Alma told us about the **insurance man** who would come to the door each Tuesday (this was around 1910) and collect a nickel for each policy. Later it was a dime, then a quarter. Eventually the policies were paid up and holders had peace of mind.

Alma passed away in the 1980s after giving us the policy that would "take care of everything." It didn't. The designated funeral home had changed hands and the policy was then valued at $250 to be applied against funeral services and burial. She had died believing the words in the document promising a rosewood casket and a ride in a hearse pulled by two white horses.

Another way to provide for the future was to pay dues to a burial or benevolent society. The better ones had large multi-vault tombs, termed "society tombs," built to accommodate members and their closest relatives. A few were sponsored by ethnic groups and provided aid to members even beyond funerals. The Zulu Social Aid and Pleasure Club was a benevolent organization that later that grew into the well-known Zulu Mardi Gras Krewe. In the distant past, similar organizations provided processions that have evolved into present-day jazz funerals.

Attitudes about honoring the dead have changed over the decades. All Saints' Day, November 1st, was once a public holiday. On that day and the day after, All Souls' Day, New Orleanians visited cemeteries, sometimes several, to bring flowers and to visit with old neighbors, friends and cousins. Not just Catholics, but locals of many faiths observed the custom. In the early twentieth century, streetcars were crowded with people visiting family gravesites. Vendors sold refreshments at the gates and it was a day of reunions among the living more than occasions of sadness. Nuns, along with a few of the children from their orphanages, would stand at the gates smiling and accepting donations.

Today, the Feast of All Saints is much more quietly observed, overshadowed by newer traditions observed on the previous night, the "Eve of All Hallows" or, as it is now known, Halloween. The tombs stand as silent reminders of simpler eras when time was taken to honor the people of the past who labored, loved and paved the way for later generations.

CHAPTER 14

St. Roch, St. Augustin and the Tomb of the Unknown Slave

Little known to tourists, St. Roch is not the oldest cemetery in New Orleans, but may be the only one started by a miracle. It was founded in 1878 by the Rev. P. L. Thevis who served a parish of German Catholic immigrants at a time when yellow fever was the most-feared scourge. He made a promise that, if none of his flock succumbed to the disease, he would build a chapel in honor of St. Roch, a fourteenth-century saint known for nursing plague victims. Since none died, it is reported, he built the chapel and surrounded it with a cemetery.

The chapel soon became the destination of New Orleanians seeking cures for a variety of ailments. As many were immigrants a generation removed from Europe, they brought religious traditions of thanking for prayers answered with mementoes. Some were simple marble plaques engraved with the word "Thanks." Others were plaster casts of healed body parts. These included feet, arms, hearts and braces that were no longer needed. All these were attached to the chapel walls as silent reminders of the successes of their prayers. In time these objects were removed to a side room but are still visible from a window, handy for viewing when the chapel is locked.

The cemetery grew to cover two city blocks and a mausoleum was added. It was favored by working class Catholic families with French, Spanish, African, Creole, German, Irish, Italian and English roots. The original cemetery space is surrounded by wall vaults punctuated, at intervals, by Stations of the Cross. On Good Fridays, even at the present time, a priest leads the faithful in prayers at each of the stations. Among the crowd may be young women who have faith in a pious superstition - the belief that if one prays for a husband at the St. Roch Cemetery on Good Friday, a suitable one will be found within the year.

St. Roch Cemetery is located on, naturally, St. Roch Avenue. It is off the beaten track for tourists but is only a ten-minute drive from the French Quarter. It contains the large Screwmen Tomb, built for a now defunct labor union made up of riverfront workers who manned large screw presses. They reduced the size of cotton bales to less than half, once vital for preparing cotton for shipment overseas.

In this cemetery are a large number of "coping" graves, almost as many as there are above ground tombs. A coping grave (they are also called coping tombs) is a small family plot surrounded by a short wall filled in with soil and topped with grass or marble chips. Some say they were developed as a way of "coping" with the desire for burials underground in an area with a high water table. Each plot features a small monument or headstone. Although they cannot accommodate as many interments as can above-ground tombs, they are adequate for many families.

The entrance gates of St. Roch are flanked by two large angel sculptures… angels with a difference. They have no wings. The wings were lost in a hurricane almost a century ago but they retain their heavenly appearance. A block away is the church of Our Lady Star of the Sea. It has a remarkable mural of eight seemingly feminine angels, each resembling the idealized beauty of each of the ethnic groups served by that church and cemetery over the years. They surround Mary, her faced damaged by Katrina. Artist Vernon Dobard hopes for funds for the scaffolding needed for restoration.

A mile and a half west of the St. Roch area and adjacent to the French Quarter is the Tremé historic neighborhood and St. Augustine Roman Catholic Church. The church has no cemetery but it does have a grave… a grave with no body. It is a monument called the Tomb of the Unknown Slave. It is not truly a tomb, but a stark reminder of the injustices of the past and is meant to honor the unmarked graves of those unlucky souls who lived and died as slaves.

The focal point is a large cross made of segments of heavy marine chain, the links welded together. Hanging from it are shackles representing the restraints used on enslaved Africans. The white wall of the church provides a dramatic background for the dark cross. Surrounding it is a well-kept garden with smaller crosses.

Saint Augustine Church was founded more than twenty years before the Civil War to serve the Catholic residents of the Tremé neighborhood. At least half of members were free persons of color and all wanted a parish church closer than the Cathedral, ten blocks distant. By tradition, half of the pews were for free persons of color and the others for persons of European descent. Slaves were seated along the sides. They all spoke French and considered themselves culturally Creole.

The Tomb of the Unknown Slave was the work of a group of parishioners and their pastor, the Rev. Jerome LeDoux, and was dedicated in 2004. Today, most of the members of the congregation are African-Americans. When Katrina struck, the flood waters surrounded the church but did not enter it or damage the symbolic tomb.

A stark reminder of the cruelty of slavery, this symbolic Grave of
the Unknown Slave is made of heavy chains hung with shackles.
It is on the side of a church in the Treme neighborhood.

Across the street from the church is the Backstreet Cultural Museum devoted to preserving the histories of the Mardi Gras Indian marching groups. These groups, composed of African Americans who make their own elaborate costumes, are a less-known part of local culture. Many of their members have been baptized, married and buried at St. Augustine.

Sunday "Jazz Masses" attract visitors from all over the city but particularly from the French Quarter. The church is often the starting point for jazz funerals, that special New Orleans way of saying the last goodbyes to musicians and well-known citizens, both black and white.

CHAPTER 15

Race and the Funeral Business

Uncle Lionel Batiste stood, nattily dressed and ramrod straight, at his own viewing. Mourners were surprised, amazed and then happy to see, one last time, the much-loved elderly drummer for the Tremé Brass Band as he had appeared in life. He had been known for walking the streets of the French Quarter and Tremé handsomely dressed and pausing to chat with friends and tourists.

Embalmed and standing up? According to the general public, it could happen only in New Orleans, a place known for quirky attitudes about death and dying. After all, where else could you find jazz funeral processions ending in dancing or people laid to rest in cemeteries resembling "cities of the dead"? It was not surprising when, two years after Uncle Lionel had been laid to rest (lying down, in a coffin), an elderly socialite, Mickey Easterling, appeared at her own wake, not standing, but sitting on a bench holding a drink in one hand and a cigarette in the other, her final appearance held in a downtown theater.

Before long, a third life-like viewing was held in another part the city. Of course, the practice did not start in New Orleans but the trend came by way of Puerto Rico. Charbonnet-Labat, the funeral home that made the news for having Uncle Batiste stand up, has been known as a provider of traditional funeral services for African-American families, many of them descendants of old-line Catholic Creoles. Mickey Easterling's sitting-up cadaver was prepared, it was said, by Schoen's on Canal Street, a castle-looking mortuary that often serves well-to-do Catholic families with European backgrounds.

Funeral homes of all kinds are busy in New Orleans. With a steady supply of deceased persons and nice facilities, they are doing well. Repaired after Hurricane Katrina's devastation, many of their properties are better than ever. About half of the city's funerals are handled by African-American-owned enterprises. These totals reflect the 50/50 racial makeup of the city.

Black families, for the most part, use the services of funeral homes catering to African-Americans while other families patronize funeral establishments primarily serving white populations. This could cynically be seen as a last remnant of segregation but the real reasons are more complex, reflecting traditions and practicality more than prejudice. Within both groups, funeral arrangement choices are often made by religious preferences, family traditions and word-of-mouth recommendations.

African-American families are loyal to funeral homes run by African-Americans, not just in New Orleans but in most communities. Many of these mortuaries are independently owned and are run by families who have been in the business for decades, some for over a century. In Jim Crow days, the funeral business was one of the few paths to prosperity for black entrepreneurs. In time, morticians became highly respected community figures, offering not only consolation for the bereaved, but civic leadership.

Black funeral businesses have roots that can be traced to the Civil War. Confederate troops were known to bring slaves to battle areas.

Some enslaved men served as assistants to medical officers, caring for the wounded and preparing bodies for burial or shipment home. It was in that war that embalming came into use. After the conflict ended, slaves who had acquired knowledge of embalming began offering services to their communities back home. By the late 1800s, African Americans were obtaining formal training and operating mortuaries.

These patterns were common across the South but particularly played a role in New Orleans where there are still a number of prominent funeral businesses begun in the late eighteen and early nineteen hundreds. They bear names like Charbonnet (dates from 1883), Rhodes (1884), Labat and Glapion. Along with more recently opened businesses, they provide services in the style and customs unique to this city.

According to Gilbert Jones of the Rhodes Funeral Home, New Orleans-style funerals in the African-American community, when compared to other funerals, tend to have a greater emphasis on the repast meal and a longer elapsed time between death and interment. Donovan Boyd of the Boyd Funeral Home was quoted in the *Dial Newspaper* on February 15, 2013, explaining that funeral homes serving African-American families provide "a greater level of comfort, and a high regard for our traditions." He went on to say, "We grieve differently and families need someone that can relate to those customs and traditions and that's why they come to us."

Well-appointed African-American Funeral Homes today are used as sites for social events that are not linked to funerals. Anniversary parties, family reunions and even wedding receptions can be held in there. Positive feelings about gatherings in these surroundings may date back to earlier days when mortuaries were safe places to gather to discuss actions to support civil rights movements.

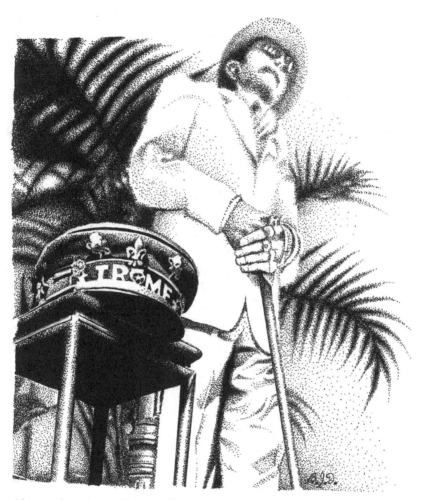

The undertaker will not tell anyone how he did it. The dead man is standing at his own wake and would have approved. Proud of his musical talent and his impeccable appearance, "Uncle" Lionel Batiste would have wanted to look his best at his last public appearance.

European descendants brought a different legacy to the funeral homes they founded. They were often outgrowths of family businesses that sold furniture back in the day when funerals were held in the home. The bereaved wanted their homes to be suitably furnished when friends visited to pay respects. A solution for many was to rent nice parlor furniture, delivered by a wagon that could also provide transportation of the deceased to the cemetery. In time, these furniture companies were providing complete undertaking services including the use of their parlors for visitations.

Long ago, the jazz funeral crossed the color line. Every local establishment now uses special mule-drawn hearses owned by the Charbonnet's for their jazz funerals. These processions, often misunderstood by outsiders, end with a celebration of the release of a person from earthly suffering and the going home to a better life. Although the jazz funerals are not an everyday event, they are the most visible local mourning custom.

Mortuaries and cemeteries primarily serving white populations are prospering but are undergoing rapid changes. Stewart Enterprises, a national organization based in the New Orleans area, had owned a large number of funeral homes and cemeteries across the U.S., including the majority of local funeral businesses serving white clients. As of this date, they are in the process of selling their holdings to Service Corporation International, a Houston-based organization, but the Federal Government may add stipulations to the sales to avoid monopolies.

African-American funeral businesses tend to be independently owned and run by families. Exceptions are the Mount Olivet Funeral Home and the adjacent Mount Olivet Cemetery which are now owned by Service Corporation International. In general, African-American funeral businesses may not generate as much profit as those catering to whites because African-American clients, on average, have lower incomes.

Cremation, pre-need planning and related insurance services are growing trends for every business providing funeral services, no matter which ethnic groups they serve. This is the case locally as well as across America. These professionals point out that it is hard for families facing the loss of a loved one to make realistic final plans, financial or otherwise. Pre-planning eases the burden and can save money.

All funeral homes and cemeteries expect full payment before burial and will advise clients of institutions that will provide loans. Funeral business that are too generous and do not insist on timely payment can find themselves... bankrupt.

People who live away from New Orleans are more likely to want to be buried in their hometown than those from other cities. It is not unheard of for cremated remains to be brought to a local cemetery to be placed in a family grave, mausoleum or tomb. It may be of interest to note that only the U.S. Post Office will ship cremains. FedEx and UPS will not knowingly handle them.

In the early years, New Orleans cemeteries were segregated by religion, not by race. When the old St. Louis Cemetery was the only one in the city, the non-Catholic newcomers were accommodated by a special annex added behind the back wall, a strip of land known as the Protestant Section. When the Girod Street Cemetery was established by the Episcopal Church shortly after the Louisiana Purchase, it too was open to all races. When it was closed in the 1950s, remains of whites and blacks were sent to separate locations. Why? No one seems to know.

City burial sites preferred by African-American families include Mount Olivet Cemetery (a choice of many affluent families, established in the 1920s), the three St. Louis Cemeteries and older neighborhood graveyards. A suburban facility, much used today, is Providence Park Cemetery and Mausoleum in Metairie (begun in the 1950s), which has the monument and burial place of Mahalia Jackson, the world-renowned gospel singer. Other than in the mausoleum, graves there are mostly in the ground.

The Charity Hospital Cemetery is the final resting place of indigent persons of all races and religions, part of which is now the Katrina Memorial. Holt Cemetery has a history of use by the poor and was once considered a "potter's field" for free burials. Now run by the city, it does not have excessive rules. It is said that a family can dig a grave for a loved one and the plot will be considered theirs as long as it is marked and maintained. The graves are below ground, many with homemade markers. Neglected, it has a certain untidy charm.

Separation by religion is still common in certain cemeteries. Hebrew cemeteries serve the Jewish population and Catholics can most often be found buried in cemeteries with saint names. Muslim families seek out a cemetery designed for them in Slidell, north of the city. In the Carrollton neighborhood is the Carrollton Cemetery which is the only city cemetery with documents showing that it was planned for separation by race when established in 1849.

Funeral directors and cemetery administrators are sensitive to the religious and cultural customs of the families who use them and are known for providing counseling, guidance and sympathy. Professionals, they would not turn away any qualifying family because of color or racial identity.

CHAPTER 16

Jazz Funerals – A Joyous Tradition

Ernie K-Doe was laid to rest in style. He was known for recording the hit rhythm & blues single "Mother-in-Law" in the 1960s. He faded from public sight for decades but was back in the musical limelight when he passed away in 2001. His jazz funeral was a bit over the top even by New Orleans standards. His lifelike wax statue was in his procession and thousands lined the route on the way to his final resting place in a donated tomb in St. Louis Cemetery No. 2.

Even more grand was the jazz funeral for Tuba Fats (Anthony Lacen) in 2004. It started at the old City Hall on St. Charles, made its way to the French Quarter and then on to Tremé. A regular at Preservation Hall, he was loved by the public and the music community. A mentor to younger jazz players, he had played on Jackson Square, in Europe and wherever his talents took him.

Not all those honored with a jazz funeral were musicians or African Americans. The popular white and long-lived retired Archbishop Philip Hannan of New Orleans had one in 2011. His jazz funeral was labeled "a solemn funeral cortege" in official press releases. It began at the seminary on Carrollton Avenue and made its way to St. Louis Cathedral accompanied by many marchers, school bands and jazz groups. The streets were lined with well-wishers. He is buried beneath the floor of the sanctuary of the St. Louis Cathedral.

A more typical jazz funeral begins at a church or funeral home. A brass band is followed by a glass-sided hearse, very likely pulled by a white mule. The flowers go on top, the coffin inside and the mourners walk behind. The procession moves slowly, dirges are played, sometimes punctuated by "A Closer Walk with Thee." Arriving at the prepared gravesite, often a tomb with a curtain hiding the empty vault, the words of religion and remembrance are said and the pallbearers lift the coffin and slide it into the tomb.

The curtain drops. The mourners realize that the cares, worries and suffering of the deceased are over. That person has gone to GLORY! The band switches to spirited music like "The Saints Go Marching In." A mood of tearful joy dawns as mourners begin to celebrate the release of their brother or sister to a better life. They follow the band, keeping time to the music, sometimes as far as to the home of the deceased. Others can join the procession, forming what is called a "second line," as even strangers can help celebrate a life.

The defining moment of a true jazz funeral is the "switch" of music from sad to joyous. With long funeral processions of local celebrities, the lively music and second line activity can make its way to the starting point. This is not perceived as disrespectful, but as a tribute, particularly by the well-organized and well-dressed marching groups that join in.

Jazz funerals have been held that do not involve a burial or prayers. Jim Monaghan's was one example. He was well known and loved in the French Quarter, had owned several drinking establishments and had sponsored parades on St. Patrick's Day. One of his last wishes was for a jazz funeral complete with a traditional hearse for his cremated remains and a band to lead the procession on a walk through the French Quarter past his favorite spots.

A Jazz Funeral is a way of celebrating a life and the release of a soul to heaven. Mournful music is played on the way to the cemetery, but after the words of prayer and the placing of the deceased into the grave, the music switches to tunes like "The Saints Go Marching In."

Not a religious man, Monaghan told his wife Liz that, if there was such a funeral, he wanted no religious music. When he passed, his friends saw to it that his wishes were carried out, hired motorcycle police to line the route, saw to the proper city permits and arranged for a first-class brass band, the Storyville Stompers.

When it was time for the event, his wife asked the band members to omit religious tunes. After a brief conference among themselves they told her that *all* jazz funeral music was religious. So the traditional music was played as Monaghan was in no position to complain. The funeral ended as he had wished, with his ashes placed above the cash register of his favorite establishment. There they remain today.

In the late 1800s, when early deaths were more frequent than today, families had a horror of being too poor to bury a loved one. Working-class people bought burial insurance at a nickel a week, collected by door-to-door insurance men. Another option was to join a mutual aid society that could provide a proper funeral. In the black community, a good "send-off" could include a procession and music.

The importance of going out in style is reflected these lines of the old blues song, "St. James Infirmary:"

"Oh, when I die, bury me
In my high top Stetson hat;
Put a twenty-dollar gold piece on my watch chain
So the boys will know I died standing pat."

Traditions evolve. A development relating to the jazz funeral is, of all things, weddings celebrated the jazz way! On a typical Saturday afternoon, there may be two of three of these happening in the French Quarter. A couple will take their vows at the St. Louis Cathedral or in

Jackson Square and have a procession to the reception led by a brass band, often the very group used in funerals. The guests become the second line, strutting and keeping time to the music.

There are other second line spin-offs, like the marching clubs seen on Mardi Gras day. Groups of men, all dressed alike, will hire a band to lead them. They will walk along the major parade routes, but not as part of any parade but simply having fun and strutting to the music, second-line style. They are known to carry sticks supporting dozens and dozens of paper flowers which they present to pretty women... in exchange for a kiss! The best known Mardi Gras marching group was founded by clarinetist Pete Fountain. It is the (pronounce it carefully) "Half-Fast Walking Society."

Scholars may not all agree that jazz was born in New Orleans, but they will admit that the word "jazz" certainly was. It was in New Orleans that it matured and became a part of the fabric of music everywhere. One wonders when the joy of jazz funeral celebrations and spirit of second line processions will spread to enrich the world scene.

Isn't every life worth celebrating?

APPENDIX I

CEMETERIES OF NEW ORLEANS: a list with suggestions for digging into the past

This book is about the thirty-five cemeteries that are within the city limits of New Orleans. I have listed them here with their addresses, founding dates and my detailed comments. It should be noted that there are modern cemeteries in nearby Jefferson Parish that are frequently used by city residents. I have saved these for another book along with descriptions of graveyards along the bayous of South Louisiana.

Following the list are two maps, one showing the locations of over a dozen cemeteries clustered at the end of the Canal/Cemeteries streetcar line. The second one shows where to find the scattered neighborhood burial grounds. Photographs for many of them can be found on the Internet. Satellite maps can afford interesting overhead views.

Respectful Visits

Cemetery authorities almost always welcome respectful tourists. Photographing is allowed. Marking on tombs is, of course, considered desecration and is illegal. Larger cemeteries allow cars to drive through slowly if they are careful to avoid funerals taking place at the time. If tombs are falling apart, don't assume neglect on the part of cemetery managers. Each grave is private property and upkeep is the job of the individual owners.

Save Our Cemeteries (SOC), www.saveourcemeteries.org, 504-525-3377, can answer questions and give updated rules. Most cemeteries publish telephone contact numbers online and in the yellow pages. For public transportation guidance try www.norta. com or phone 504-248-3900. Streetcar and bus fares are $1.25. Taxicab costs are reasonable.

The burial grounds are in alphabetical order in each sub-section. A tour led by a professional guide is a good first step for exploring "The Cities of the Dead." Many tour companies offer them on a regular basis. Tips for exploring these sites on your own are given at the end of this list.

The St. Louis Cemeteries

Of the three cemeteries below, only St. Louis Cemetery No. 2 may be open for walk-in visitors, but this may change. For information about them and others managed by the Catholic Archdiocese of New Orleans, click to www.NOLAcatholiccemeteries.org or phone 504-596-3050.

It should be noted that, although it is not a cemetery, there have been burials of bishops and other notables both in and behind the St. Louis Cathedral, 700 Chartres.

1. **St. Louis Cemetery No. 1**, 425 Basin Street, was founded in 1789 and is the oldest in the city and possibly the most interesting. It has graves of Marie Laveau, Homer Plessy and heroes of the Battle of New Orleans. Catholic, it has a separate section for Protestants. The provocative *Easy Rider* scenes shot there in 1969 led to a decades-old ban on commercial filming in local Catholic cemeteries. Many companies offer daily tours and, since it is not now open to the public, taking an escorted tour may be the only way to gain entrance. (See tour in Chapter 1)Tomb owners and their families are, of course, given access.

2. **St. Louis Cemetery No. 2**, 320 N. Claiborne Avenue, was founded in 1823. It has few visitors so is best seen with a group. It is rich in history and architectural styles and has tombs of the pirate Dominique You, Blessed Henriette Delille, musicians and notable Creole families.

3. **St. Louis Cemetery No. 3**, 3421 Esplanade Avenue, was founded in 1854. It is near City Park and has become a popular stop for bus tours. Large and well kept, it has a variety of family and monumental tombs, a large Greek Orthodox structure, mausoleums and an office with records of the three St. Louis Cemeteries. A new feature, located near the main gate, is a structure specifically designed to hold cremated remains.

The intersection where Canal Street meets City Park Avenue is surrounded by over a dozen graveyards and is a busy transfer point for people using public transportation. Once it was at the edge of the inhabited part of the city, the land beyond it swampy until drained in the early 1900s. As the land dried, it began to be used for residential housing and a large suburb called Lakeview. (It should be noted that Katrina waters flooded Lakeview in 2005 but spared much of the cemeteries area.)

The Canal/Cemeteries Streetcar ends at the cemeteries. As you face the Elk Monument, even-numbered cemetery addresses on Canal Street will be on your left. Turning right to City Park Avenue, even numbered sites will be on the right. You may want to avail yourself of nearby coffee shops at 5045 Canal Street and 5201 Canal Boulevard, the name of the extension of Canal Street.

4. **Charity Hospital Cemetery**, 5050 Canal Street, was founded 1847 and contains thousands of unmarked below-ground graves of the poor. The Katrina National Memorial Park now occupies the most visible part of the area, just within the gate. It has six structures containing the bodies of unclaimed Katrina victims that encircle the area in an artful simulation of hurricane winds. (See chapter 7.) It, like most local cemeteries, is open daily.

5. **Chevra Thilim/Beth Israel/Gates of Prayer Cemeteries**, 4824 Canal Street. Gates of Prayer was established in 1846 and is considered the oldest existing Jewish burial ground in New Orleans. The wrought-iron gate on Canal Street says "Chevra Thilim Cemetery Assn." Jewish congregations enlarged the burial ground at later dates. One of these has a lighthouse monument honoring a supporter of the Lighthouse for

the Blind. The combined cemetery wraps partly around a former funeral home which is now used for other purposes including receptions and Halloween events. As with other local Hebrew cemeteries, burial is below ground and of the coping style. Most graves face eastward toward Jerusalem and have fairly modest monuments. Records are housed in a synagogue in Jefferson Parish.

6. **Chevra Thilim Memorial Park Cemetery,** 500 Iberville Street, was founded in 1973. It is the newest and smallest Jewish cemetery and adjoins Dispersed of Judah Cemetery. It has uniform graves all facing east.

7. **Cypress Grove Cemetery,** 120 City Park Avenue, corner Canal Street, was established in 1840 by the Firemen's Charitable and Benevolent Association. It has interesting examples of memorial art and a structure once used as a holding tomb for bodies of Chinese immigrants awaiting burial in their native land.

8. **Dispersed of Judah Cemetery,** 4937 Canal Street, was begun in 1847 and is the second oldest Jewish cemetery in New Orleans. It has a large stone in honor of Judah Touro, philanthropist and founder of Touro Hospital. Older grave markers have Hebrew inscriptions.

9. **Greenwood Cemetery,** located where City Park Avenue meets Canal Street, was opened in 1852 by the Firemen's Charitable & Benevolent Association. Very large, it has twelve acres of closely placed family tombs and a mausoleum. Prominent monuments overlooking the end of the Canal Streetcar line include a large memorial honoring firefighters who died in the line of duty and a mound topped by a large sculpture of an elk guarding graves of members of the Fraternal Order of

Elks. Far to the left is a touching memorial to the Confederate dead and an interstate highway.

10. **Holt Cemetery**, 635 City Park Avenue, was opened in 1879 for the indigent, is now managed by the City of New Orleans. Most of the burials are below ground. The markers include some that are homemade and are fine examples of folk art. Affordable, it is said that plots are owned by families as long as they are maintained. It is located to the right and across a railroad track from St. Patrick Cemetery No. 3. The entrance is hard to spot because it is set back behind a bordering wall. Enter via Buddy Bolden Street off City Park Avenue. If you reach Delgado Community College, you've gone too far but are handy to a well-liked hamburger restaurant.

11. **Lake Lawn Park Cemetery** and Mausoleum, 5454 Pontchartrain Boulevard, was established in 1949. To enter, follow City Park Avenue west to the interstate highway, cross under it, go right carefully watching for cars, and continue alongside the adjacent Metairie Cemetery, their partner organization, and follow the sidewalk and pass under the railroad tracks. (The entrance is a good half mile north of City Park Avenue. Think about taking a car or taxi.) Both it and Metairie Cemetery are owned by Service Corporation International. There are not many tombs but there is a large mausoleum with stained glass windows.

12. **Masonic Cemetery No. 1**, 400 City Park Avenue, was founded in 1865 and built with contributions from several Masonic Lodges. It has some unusual group tombs and a number of epitaphs, a feature rare in New Orleans. Notable is a multi-vault tomb with steps leading to the roof. **Masonic Cemetery No. 2** dates from the late 1860s. Like No. 1, it is

rich in Masonic symbolism, but has more modest graves. It is separated from Masonic Cemetery No. 1 by Conti Street.

13. **Metairie Cemetery**, 5100 Pontchartrain Boulevard, was established in 1873 on the site of a former racetrack. Although there is a suburb called Metairie, this cemetery is within New Orleans city limits. It is the final resting place of the elite and has a wealth of outstanding and beautifully designed monuments. An adjacent mausoleum features religious-themed artwork and stained glass. A funeral home on the grounds will provide visitors with self-guided tour materials. See directions above to Lake Lawn Cemetery. Metairie Cemetery is somewhat closer and much larger. At the corner of Pontchartrain Boulevard and City Park Avenue (renamed Metairie Road at this point), there is a handy gate for pedestrians. The gates for automobiles are all on Pontchartrain Boulevard and driving through is permitted.

14. **Odd Fellows Rest**, 5055 Canal Street, Corner of City Park Avenue, was founded in 1849 by a charitable society whose membership was secret and not a part of any religious organization. Members of the society were known for helping during yellow fever epidemics. A number of black families have tombs there. At this time it is kept locked but it can be viewed through the gates or from an adjoining cemetery.

15. **St. John/Hope Mausoleum**, 4841 Canal Street, began in 1867 as a Lutheran cemetery, the second-oldest Protestant one in the city (Girod Street Cemetery, now gone, was the first, founded in 1822). It became non-sectarian in 1931 when a mausoleum was added which now wraps partially around it.

16. **St. Patrick Cemetery No. 1**, 5040 Canal Street, was founded in 1840 for Irish immigrants. Many died of yellow fever while working on a nearby canal. When closed, the canal space

was used to build part of the nearby interstate highway. It has a number of simple tombs and coping graves, a small mausoleum in the rear and is next to the Charity Hospital Cemetery. **St. Patrick Cemetery No. 2**, 142 City Park Avenue, founded 1841, has more elaborate family tombs and a bit more decay than the other two cemeteries of the same name. It borders Canal Street across from St. Patrick Cemetery No. 1. The other end borders City Park Avenue across from St. Patrick Cemetery No. 3. From the air, the three cemeteries seem to form one long strip of land separated by public streets. **St. Patrick Cemetery No. 3**, 143 City Park Avenue, has an uncertain founding date but it may have been in the early 1850s. It has an office, an open-style mausoleum and statues of St. Patrick and Pope John XXIII. All three St. Patrick Cemeteries have Stations of the Cross figures at the gates.

Uptown Cemeteries (Southwest of Canal Street)

After the Louisiana Purchase, English and German-speaking newcomers flooded into New Orleans and settled upriver from the old French-speaking part of the city, hence the term "uptown." A reminder of that settlement pattern is the fact that today streets change their names as they cross Canal Street, the old dividing line.

The newcomers came with less immunities to yellow fever than the original population. Burial dates in the cemeteries reflect epidemics. Infected adults usually died but children often survived so the uptown area had several orphanages. The Lafayette Cemetery has a well-marked tomb for orphans.

Locations below include the Garden District and Carrollton areas. A city map or GPS is helpful in finding these quaint neighborhood graveyards. Each one is fairly accessible to the St. Charles Avenue Streetcar line. The fare is $1.25 plus transfers. Driving through may be allowed.

17. **Carrollton Cemetery**, 1701 Hillary Street, was founded by immigrants in 1848 when Carrollton was a separate town. Unlike its predecessors in New Orleans, it was designed for racial separation with designated areas for white and black families. Now it is administered by the city and has a new iron fence. It was once neglected but now shows signs of improvement.

18. **Gates of Prayer Cemetery No. 2**, 2422 Joseph Street, was begun in 1853. Jewish, it has modern below-ground graves, a few monuments and an unusual collection of old tombstones with Hebrew inscriptions. It is carefully maintained. The small stones placed on some of the markers reflect a traditional way that visitors show respect for the departed.

19. **Lafayette Cemetery No. 1**, 1400 Washington Avenue, was begun in 1833 in the town of Lafayette, now a part of New Orleans known as the Garden District. It is similar to ones found in Creole neighborhoods. Some above-ground tombs are quite fashionable, patterned after Parisian graves. It is fairly well-kept and attracts a good number of tourists, some looking for sites mentioned in novels by Anne Rice. Tours are offered by several companies. The Save Our Cemeteries organization has been active in preserving the site. Refreshments can be found nearby at the corner of Washington and Prytania streets.

20. **Lafayette Cemetery No. 2**, 2200 Washington Avenue, was established 1851. Both Lafayette Cemeteries are administered by the City of New Orleans and are twelve blocks apart.

Once neglected, it is improving. It can now be locked at night because of a new black metal fence—a fence which distinguishes it from the adjacent St. Joseph Cemeteries, which have chain link fences. Questionable neighborhood.

21. **St. Mary Cemetery**, 2000 Hillary Street, was founded 1849. Once a church cemetery, it is now administered by the city and is undergoing improvements. It is near the Carrollton Cemetery. (There is also a St. Mary Cemetery on the West Bank of New Orleans; no connection.)

22. **St. Joseph Cemetery No. 1**, 2220 Washington Avenue, was established in 1854 by a religious order of nuns who sold plots to help support their orphanage. The cemetery is now administered by the Catholic Archdiocese of New Orleans and has variety of tombs. It is next to both Lafayette Cemetery No. 2 and **St. Joseph Cemetery No. 2**, established 1873. It has many coping graves, few tombs. One gothic-style, monumental tomb with stained glass stands out.

23. **Ursuline Mortuary Chapel**, constructed in 1924, holds remains of Ursuline nuns from the 1700s to the present time. Private, it is located within the grounds of Ursuline Academy at 2635 State Street. Call ahead for permission to visit at 504-861-9150. (See mention in Chapters 8 and 11.

24. **Valence Cemetery**, 2000 Valence Street, was founded in 1867. Like many small cemeteries run by the city, it was once neglected but is now better kept. It has a new iron fence and crumbling graves. As with all cemeteries, upkeep of graves is the responsibility of the families that own them. In the case of tombs that are over a century old, the families may have forgotten about them, moved away or died out.

25. **St. Vincent de Paul Cemetery No. 1**, 1950 Soniat Street, was founded in 1859 and is administered by the Catholic

Archdiocese of New Orleans. Clean and fairly well maintained, it contains many traditional tombs. (Not to be confused with the St. Vincent de Paul Cemeteries numbered one, two and three that are located downriver. Those have no church affiliation.) **St. Vincent de Paul Cemetery No. 2** was founded 1889 as an extension. It has brick walls, a small mausoleum and graves described in an interesting article by R. Stephanie Bruno, "At St. Vincent de Paul Cemetery, Eternal Homes Hold Architectural Interest." It was printed in the Times-Picayune newspaper, October 28, 2011.

Downriver Cemeteries (East of Canal Street)

There are five Jewish cemeteries clustered on Elysian Fields Avenue that can be easily reached by the Elysian Fields bus. These five did not flood at the time of Hurricane Katrina as they are located on the higher ground known as the Metairie-Gentilly Ridge, once the path of a bayou. Each one reflects a different tradition.

Mount Olivet is within walking distance of the Jewish cemeteries and is nonsectarian. Other cemeteries mentioned below are further east and can be reached by public bus lines.

26. **Agudath Achim Anshe Sfard Cemetery**, 4400 Elysian Fields Avenue, was opened in 1896. Founded by Russian and Polish Jews, it has special markers on graves of Holocaust survivors.
27. **Congregation Beth Israel Cemetery**, 4221 Frenchman Street, was founded in 1904 by a merger of several small Orthodox Jewish organizations. After Katrina flooded their Orthodox synagogue, damaged copies of the Torah were buried there in accordance with custom.

28. **Hebrew Rest No. 1**, 4100 Elysian Fields Avenue, was opened in 1860 and contains the remains of the city's first Jewish burial ground, Gates of Mercy, which was demolished in 1957. Adjacent is **Hebrew Rest No. 2**, 4100 Frenchmen Street, was established in 1894 and has some elaborate monuments. **Hebrew Rest No. 3**, 4200 Frenchmen Street, was begun in 1938. It has a mausoleum and an interesting marker depicting Mr. Bingle, a well-known local puppet figure, on the grave of the man who developed it. Records for Hebrew Rest Numbers One, Two and Three are located at Temple Sinai Reform Congregation on St. Charles Avenue. The three combined are considered the largest Jewish burial ground in the city.

29. **Mount Olivet**, 400 Norman Mayer Avenue, was established in the 1920s for elite black and Creole families and has traditional tombs, below-ground burials and a mausoleum. It is now owned and operated by Service Corporation International, a large, for-profit organization. The location is near Dillard University.

30. **Rest Haven Memorial Park**, 10400 Old Gentilly Road, was named Lincoln Park Cemetery until the 1930s. The founding date is unknown. Small, it is the furthest east of all New Orleans cemeteries and caters to African-American families. Most burials are below ground.

31. **St. Roch Cemetery No. 1**, 1725 St. Roch Ave, was founded 1874 by a German Catholic pastor. It contains a chapel with mementoes for prayers answered. Wall vault sections alternate with sculptured scenes of the Stations of the Cross. (More about it can be found in Chapter 14.) **St. Roch Cemetery No. 2** is separated from No. 1 by Music Street. It was opened in 1895 and has family tombs and a combined

chapel and mausoleum. Both cemeteries are operated by the Archdiocese of New Orleans.

32. **St. Vincent de Paul Cemetery No. 1** (also called Louisa Street Cemetery), 1322 Louisa Street, was established 1838 to serve the needs of Creoles and immigrants. It was once owned by a fencing master (an untrue legend is that it was for persons killed in duels). **St. Vincent de Paul Cemetery No. 2** is adjacent to St. Vincent de Paul No. 1. The founding date may be near 1838. It is separated from St. Vincent de Paul No. 1 by Piety Street. The founding year of **St. Vincent de Paul Cemetery No. 3** is assumed to be after 1838. It is fairly well kept as are the other two cemeteries, all owned by Service Corporation International. Their history is clouded but despite their names there is no evidence that they were ever church cemeteries. Each is on a separate square but share the same address. There are two cemeteries by the same name located uptown that are administered by the Catholic Archdiocese of New Orleans. Confusing!

West Bank (Algiers) Cemeteries

Counties in Louisiana (called "parishes") that are located along the Mississippi River have sections on both the east and west banks. In the early days, it was easier to cross the river than to travel on land. A picturesque way to reach some of the cemeteries on the West Bank of New Orleans, the part of the city called Algiers, is by ferry - but the Mississippi River Bridge can take you there as well. From the ferry landing, take Bouny Street south to Nunez Street for the St. Mary and St. Bartholomew cemeteries. There are good coffee stops along the way. Finding Eureka Lodge Cemetery, further east, will require a car and patience.

33. **Eureka Lodge Cemetery**, located at Boyd and Ivory Streets, may have been founded in the 1970s or earlier. Most graves are below ground and somewhat overgrown. It is a good distance east (about 5 miles) from the ferry landing.

34. **St. Bartholomew Cemetery** is located where Nunez meets Lamarque Street. It was founded as early as 1848, the founding date of the Holy Name of Mary Church in Algiers which administers it. Unlike Catholic churches on the East Bank, it is not managed by the Archdiocese of New Orleans. Burial records are incomplete. Some tombs are 150 years old. Neatly maintained, it features a huge cross with a bleeding figure of Christ.

35. **St. Mary Cemetery**, found on Nunez at De Armas Street, was founded in 1866, perhaps as a smaller extension of St. Bartholomew. It is also run by the Holy Name of Mary Catholic Parish. Both cemeteries are a healthy ten-block walk from the ferry landing. Like St. Bartholomew's, most of the graves are traditional family tombs, copings and society tombs. Note: there is also a St. Mary Cemetery on the East Bank.

The Algiers area also contains a number of scattered unlisted and half-hidden graveyards, many begun by small churches at a time when the West Bank was composed of rural communities.

Dead Cemeteries, Gone Forever:

Duverje Cemetery was founded in 1818 as a private chapel and burial ground for family members, servants and slaves. It was on a triangle of land between Verret and Seguin streets. In 1917, the remains of plantation family members and the large granite Duverje tomb were moved to Metairie Cemetery. Future research may reveal if slave remains were moved to Metairie Cemetery as well. Heirs donated the old cemetery land to the Algiers community to become the Delcazal Park for children.

Gates of Mercy, formerly at Saratoga and Jackson Avenue, was founded in 1828 and was the city's first Jewish Cemetery. Now demolished, the graves were moved in 1957 to Hebrew Rest Cemetery in Gentilly and the space is now a playground.

Girod Street Cemetery, established in 1822 on Girod Street, was the first Protestant cemetery in New Orleans. It was deconsecrated and torn down in 1957. The site is now covered by part of a defunct shopping area and a section of the Superdome parking lot. (See chapters 8 and 9.)

The Bayou St. John Cemetery was in use, according to death records, by 1835. No one seems to have been interred there after the 1840s (officially, anyway). The exact former location is unknown today but it is assumed, because of its name, to have been near the Bayou St. John.

The St. Peter Street Cemetery, once near St. Peter and Burgundy Streets in the French Quarter, was deconsecrated a few years after the first St. Louis Cemetery (1789) came into use. Remains were moved to the new burial ground but recent building projects revealed that some bodies were left behind.

Helpful Hints for Cemetery Explorations

    a. Have a goal, but make it flexible: you may want to change focus as you make discoveries.

b. Themes make it interesting. For example: types of decorative iron, tomb architecture, ethnic names, comparisons of religious customs, symbolism, graves of celebrities or historic figures, curious or outstanding monuments or epitaphs (hard to find on local graves).

c. Bring a camera or cell phone that takes good photographs, a notepad and drinking water. (New Orleans' tap water is quite good and cemeteries have faucets but somehow drinking graveyard water does not appeal.)

d. Use common sense. The dead won't hurt you but living persons could. Crime in cemeteries is rare, however. Safety while visiting them depends on the neighborhood and the number of other visitors present.

e. Consider going with a buddy or group. Stay in fairly close proximity to each other or you will be slowed down by distance shouts of "Look at this" which you will feel compelled check out. Exploring with others adds to the experience, particularly if you stop from time to time for refreshments and note sharing.

f. Dress for the weather, which can change from hour to hour in New Orleans.

g. Wear comfortable shoes, not thongs (oops… today they call them flip-flops).

h. Research done both before and after cemetery visits can yield treasures of information. There are many good printed and Internet resources. Experiment with search terms.

i. Bring this book with you!

APPENDIX II

Maps

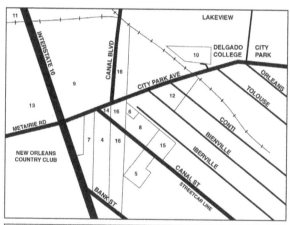

MAP KEY:

1. Saint Louis No. 1
2. Saint Louis No. 2
3. Saint Louis No. 3
4. Charity Hospital, Katrina Cemetery
5. Cevra Thilim, Beth Israel Gates of Prayer Cem.
6. Cevra Thilim Mem. Cem.
7. Cypress Grove Cemetery
8. Dispersed of Judah Cem.
9. Greenwood Cemetery
10. Holt Cemetery
11. Lake Lawn Park Cem.
12. Masonic Cem. No. 1,2
13. Metairie Cemetery
14. Odd Fellows Rest
15. St John/Hope Maus.
16. St. Patrick No. 1,2,3
17. Carrollton Cemetery
18. Gates of Prayer No. 2
19. Lafayette Cem. No. 1
20. Lafayette No. 2
21. St. Mary Cemetery
22. St. Joseph No. 1,2
23. Ursuline Mort. Chapel
24. Valence Cemetery
25. St. Vincent No. 1,2,3
26. Agudath Anse Sfard
27. Cong. Beth Israel Cem.
28. Hebrew Rest No. 1,2,3
29. Mount Olivet Cem.
30. Resthaven Mem. Park
31. Saint Roch No. 1,2
32. St. Vincent No. 1,2,3
33. Eureka Lodge Cem.
34. St. Bartholomew
35. St. Mary Cemetery

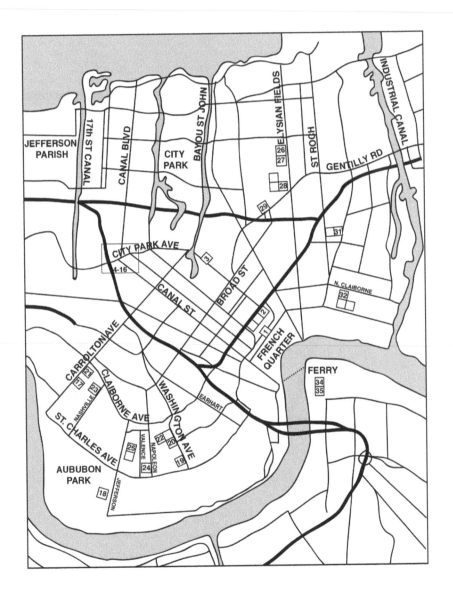

APPENDIX III

Resources

Books and Articles

Burst, Deborah, *Louisiana's Scared Places: Churches, Cemeteries and Voodoo*, Cloud Burst Publishing, 2014.

Carll, Angela, *Where the Writers Wrote in New Orleans*, Margaret Media, Inc., 2013.

Campanella, Richard, *Time and Place in New Orleans*, Pelican Publishing Company, 2002.

Christovich, Mary Louise, *New Orleans Architecture, Volume III: The Cemeteries*, Friends of the Cabildo and Pelican Publishing Company, 1974 and 1977.

Culbertson, Judi and Randall, Tom, *Permanent Parisians*, Chelsea Green Publishing, 1986.

Daughty, Caitlin, *Smoke Gets In Your Eyes, And Other Lessons from the Crematory*, Barnes and Noble, 2014.

Gehman, Mary, *The Free People of Color of New Orleans*, Margaret Media, Inc., 1994.

Florence, Robert, *City of the Dead: A Journey Through St. Louis Cemetery #1, New Orleans, Louisiana,* University of Southwestern Louisiana, 1996.

Florence, Robert and Mason Florence, *New Orleans Cemeteries: Life in the City of the Dead,* Batture Press, 1995.

Gandolfo, Henri: *Metairie Cemetery: An Historical Memoir* Published by Stewart Enterprises Inc. 1981 and 1998.

Hannah, Lindsay, editor, *Tomb It May Concern: Tour Guide Training Manual,* Save Our Cemeteries, Inc., 2008.

Long, Carolyn Morrow, *Madame Lalaurie, Mistress of the Haunted House,* University Press of Florida, 2012.

Manhein, Mary H., *Trail of Bones: More Cases from the Files of a Forensic Anthropologist,* Published by Louisiana State University Press, 2003

Mitford, Jessica, *The American Way of Death,* Fawcett Crest, 1977.

Mueller, Tom, "CSI: Italian Renaissance," *Smithsonian Magazine* article, July-August, 2013.

Roach, Mary, *Stiff: The Curious Lives of Human Cadavers,* W.W. Norton & Company, 2003.

Taylor, Michael L., "The Civil War Experiences of a New Orleans Undertaker," *Louisiana History: Journal of the Louisiana Historical Association,* Volume LV, No, 3, Summer 2014.

Suggested Internet Sources:

www.findagrave.com
www.la-cemeteries.com (click on parish, then Orleans)
www.saveourcemeteries.org
www.iajgsjewishcemeteryproject.org

Don't be afraid to experiment with terms and cemetery names on Internet search engines. There is a wealth of information and photographs, but it can take patience and detective work. Try Google Earth for satellite images that give rather detailed overhead views.

The best information can come from actual visits to cemeteries: walking in them and talking to people, there and elsewhere. When it comes to graves, no one is a stranger.

APPENDIX IV

Index

R

relics 37–38
Rhodes Funeral Home 78
Rice, Anne 24, 97
rigor mortis 12

S

Saints Go Marching In 84–85
Santeria 24
Save Our Cemeteries x, 61, 90, 97, 108
Second Line 84, 87
Short, Jonte 33
shrouds 50, 53
six feet under 51, 56
society tombs 7, 69, 102
St. Augustine 73, 75
St. Bernard Parish 27
St. James Infirmary 86
Storyville Stompers 86
St. Roch 71–73, 100
Superdome 2, 47–48, 103

T

Tennessee Williams 8
Tomb of the Unknown Slave 71, 73
Tremé Brass Band 76

U

Ursuline Sisters 36, 52
U.S. Army Corps of Engineers 28

V

vandals 18, 21, 24–25
Villarrubia ix, 38, 60, 65–68
Voodoo 1–2, 21–24, 107

W

wrought iron 60

Z

zombie 24

ABOUT THE AUTHOR

Mary LaCoste is a native of New Orleans with a successful retirement career as a tour guide and journalist. Over the years she has served as a teacher, principal and university instructor. She spent several years in Europe and Pennsylvania and returned home with a renewed appreciation of the unique history and customs of her city.

Fascinated by the tomb owned by her husband's family and determined to set the record straight for visitors and her many grandchildren, she began the long process of seeking out information through personal inquiry and research sources.

A volunteer with local preservation groups, she helps organize and give stained glass tours of local houses of worship. She holds a Doctor of Education degree from the University of New Orleans and is a member of the Ursuline Academy Alumnae Association.